The Prodigal Father

Stories of God's prodigal grace

David Marshall

The Prodigal Father

'In God there is no unChristlikeness at all. If you think there is, it is because you have misunderstood something.'

Michael Ramsey

First published in 2010

British Library Cataloguing in Publication Data.
A catalogue record for this book is available from the British Library.

ISBN 978-1-906381-87-5

Published by Autumn House (Europe), Grantham, Lincolnshire.

Designed by Abigail Murphy.

Printed in Thailand.

Unless otherwise stated, texts are taken from the *New International Version* (Hodder and Stoughton) of the Bible.

Other versions used, indicated by initials:
NLT = *New Living Translation* (Tyndale)
MGE = *The Message* by Eugene Peterson (NavPress)
NEB = *New English Bible* (Oxford)
Phillips = *New Testament in Modern English* by J. B. Phillips (Bles)
NASB = *New American Standard Bible* (Holman)
NRSV = *New Revised Standard Version* (Oxford)
The Clear Word by Jack Blanco (Review and Herald)

Contents

Upfront. The prodigal of the parable 4

1. Scandalous! 7
2. Outrageous! 11
3. Saving grace 15
4. The lure of the Far Country 20
5. The welcoming Father 23
6. The true Elder Brother 28
7. The place of brokenness 31
8. Love is the proof 34
9. A Lamb at Passover 38
10. Men caught in hypocrisy 42
11. The Champion who fights our battles 46
12. Zero to hero. Then down-down-down! 50
13. Making sure the connection is *alive* 54
14. The making of a hero 58
15. Grace like a river 63
16. Time to break cover 67
17. Being gracious is more important than being right 73
18. Grace as power 78
19. The rainbow of grace 83
20. The prodigal daughter story 89
21. Grace: The source of the miracle 94
22. When grace comes to Roaring Camp 97
23. God coming through 104

Conclusion. The invitation of grace 108

Upfront

The prodigal of the parable

We tend to give the younger brother the starring role in the Lost Son narrative.

The story starts with his sullen, unfeeling demand that he be given his share of the family estate right away. We note that a younger brother's share was normally a third of net worth, available only on the father's death. We pause to take in the thought that he wants his father's things, but not his father. Indeed, that he wants those things so badly, apparently, that he cannot wait around for his father to die. He is impatient for that event.

We contemplate the hurting heart of the father, and wonder what measures he would have taken to raise the cash equivalent of one-third of his estate. Sale? Remortgaging? Perhaps we wonder why the rejection experienced by the father does not provoke him, in turn, to reject his younger son. Why does he absorb the loss of honour and actually give the callous cad what he wants?

We picture the youth in the casinos and red-light joints of the Far Country, wasting his father's hard-earned fortune. Then the bankruptcy of the flint-hearted absconder, and the famished state that reduces him to salivating at the sight of pigswill. Then his sudden recovery of sound sense, followed by his returning – penniless and penitent – to seek employment from the father he has abandoned.

We make the wastrel's return the climactic scene of the production. The father – running. The father – embracing the scamp. The father – interrupting, before the boy can ask for a job, to take him back as a son and heir. The fade-out occurs at the height of the party, with the father's saying, 'For this my son was dead and is alive; was lost and is found.'

Told in this way, the story is powerful and valid. But if the son is the focus of every scene, then a vital perspective is lost. Certainly, the story is incomplete. We have left out the main character. We have also left out a character who represents those whom Jesus targeted by telling the story.

Neither son is the main character. Both sons are, in some sense, prodigal, but not nearly as prodigal as the father. This is the story of the Prodigal Father.

The father's character is at its heart. The younger son's initiatives and desires are almost stereotypical. The totally surprising actions in the story are those of the father. The son wants to leave with his share of the family fortune; the father, without rejecting him, permits it. The son wants to return to the homestead for paid employment; the father runs to meet him, sweeps him up in a warm embrace while the stink of the pigsty is still on him, arranges for him to be shod, demands that the ring of sonship be placed on his finger and that the 'best robe' (doubtless the father's own) be brought from the house and placed about his shoulders. Finally, a revel to end all revels is thrown to celebrate the homecoming.

It is when the party is in full swing that the older brother returns from his work. He becomes the second son to disgrace his father.

Jesus tells his three 'lost' stories – the Lost Sheep, the Lost Coin and the Lost Son (Luke 15) – when 'large crowds' are travelling with him (14:25). The Pharisees, looking down their noses, complain that the crowds contain a disproportionate number of 'sinners' and disreputable types. And, worse, that Jesus is 'welcoming' them and even 'eating with them' (15:2). It is just then that Jesus starts in on his first story.

It is not until Jesus reaches the second part of his third story (15:25-32) that he deals with the Pharisees' complaint. Not to consider the outrageous behaviour of the older son, the tender way in which the father speaks to him and the unsatisfactory way in which the story ends, would be to omit something of great importance.

Jesus does not say so, but God is the Father in this story.

The younger son is the one who is, in our terms, 'bad'. By contrast, his older brother is, in our terms, 'good'. He has (his word) 'slaved' for his father and has meticulously obeyed his every 'order'.

Nevertheless, the return of his wastrel brother brings out an anger and alienation in his character that must always have been there. He refuses to be part of the celebration for one whom he continues to regard as a cad. He has been obsessive in his obedience to the rules of the household and wants to use his record of rectitude to employ moral blackmail. He has his 'rights'! Among them, apparently, is the right to the ultimate place of favour. Another is the right to tell the father what to do with his rings, robes, livestock – and his love and favour.

At one level, the older brother is a Pharisee. At another, he stands for legalistic Christians. The problem with legalism is that it is based on DIY salvation. Legalists misconstrue both sin and salvation. Sin is more than rule-breaking. Righteousness is more than rule-keeping.

We are uncomfortable with how the story ends because the 'good' brother is angry, alienated and outside.

Jesus has been addressing himself to religious people. As the story concludes, they are outside the party, blind to the reality that only the father's grace can give them salvation. We leave them still demanding their 'rights'.

But, hey, the father has followed his invitation to enter by leaving the door ajar.

Note: The story of the Lost Son, as Jesus told it, is recorded in Luke's gospel chapter 15 verses 11-32.

1

Scandalous!

As a king, David was at the top of his game. As a man, he was at the peak of his potency.

David's commander-in-chief, Joab, was leading his armies in the siege of the Ammonite capital, Rabbah (now called Amman).

Where was David?

Back home in Jerusalem. It was late afternoon on a spring day and he was just waking up from a snooze.

Having nothing in particular to do, David took a stroll on the flat roof of his palace.

'From the roof he saw a woman bathing. The woman was very beautiful. . . .'[1]

And from the time David saw Bathsheba in the shower to the time, perhaps a year later, when he encountered the prophet Nathan, Israel's king lived like an atheist. Lust can do that to a person. So can anger, bitterness, resentment, unforgiveness, the pursuit of money, the pursuit of power, and a great many other things.

God doesn't go anywhere, of course. But driven by lust, anger, bitterness, whatever, the person behaves as if there is no God.

When you come right down to it, that is what atheism is: *living as if there is no God*. That being the case, most of us have been guilty of it at one time or another.

An individual's *actions* indicate to us whether he or she is an atheist. We have only actions to go by.

We cannot know whether the person sitting next to us is an atheist. We cannot enter into his or her thought processes. We cannot rely on his or her words. We have only his or her actions to go by.

An atheist is someone who conducts his life as if there were no God. His actions betray his atheism.

I have known many pew-sitting atheists in my time. I have known a surprising number of pew-sitting spiritual schizophrenics, and a few of the spiritually bi-polar. But these conditions are suggested by patterns of behaviour indicative that, for the time being, the sufferer is living independently of the principles and power of God.

For the time being God's existence was ignored by David, King of Israel, and his plans, principles and purposes were not taken into account.

A man of 50, David was behaving like an adolescent. Eyes wide, jaw dropped, the besotted king was engrossed by the sight of a woman far less than half his age taking a shower in her back yard. His eyes were almost out of their sockets, and his tongue was hanging out.

Apparently unaware that he was being pathetic, the king summoned someone to join him. In effect, he told him: 'Hey! Go check *her* out!'

The 50-year-old king was like an adolescent checking out 'the talent' at the beginning of term, too excited to call over himself.

'The man said, "Isn't this Bathsheba, the daughter of Eliam and the wife of Uriah the Hittite?" '

That should have served as warning enough. But David, looking at Bathsheba, had his back turned to God. His behaviour was contemptible.

'Then David sent messengers to get her. She came to him, and he slept with her. . . . Then she went back home.'

By any standards, that's far from being a love story. It was a squalid one-night stand. An attractive young woman, someone else's wife, whom the king didn't know and who had no choice in the matter, was used and then discarded.

Having summoned someone to identify Bathsheba and someone to fetch her, it is most unlikely that the King's one-night stand was a secret. He may have thought it was, but his inner circle knew what had happened.

The courtier sent to identify Bathsheba had, in effect, said to the King (see verse 3): 'Don't you realise that that attractive young woman is the daughter of one of your finest warriors and the wife of another? *Do you really want to be guilty of betrayal on that scale?*' Both Eliam and Uriah are listed among the military heroes of David's reign.[2] The courtier could have added that Bathsheba was also the granddaughter of David's senior advisor and friend, Ahithophel.

David had ignored the warning. He was in atheistic mode. Lust was in the driving seat. The only fact about Uriah that mattered to him was his absence.

That might have been the end of the story had it not been for a message David received from Bathsheba sometime later: 'I am pregnant.'

Suddenly Uriah became important to David. And it was important to David that Uriah was *present*, not *absent*. David was his own spin-doctor. He would summon Uriah back from the Eastern front for one night, and he could be held responsible for the pregnancy. So messengers were dispatched from Jerusalem, down the Jericho road, across Jordan and the Eastern desert to Amman where Joab's armies were stationed. Uriah was sought out and summoned back to base. He began the long, punishing journey up mountain, wondering what it was all about.

When, after a long ride, Uriah arrived at court in Jerusalem, the atmosphere was stiff and stilted: 'David asked if Joab was well and if the army was well and if the war was going well,' and 'Uriah replied, "Well!" '[3] Perhaps Uriah wondered why the normally affable king was so awkward in his company.

Atheistic mode notwithstanding, it's possible that David's conscience kicked in at this point.

After being debriefed, Uriah was urged to go home and relax.

Perhaps David's wink was suggestive. Whether he winked or not, he certainly sent a servant after Uriah with a gift. 'Flowers for the lady?'

David was in atheistic mode. Uriah was not. He was as high-principled as ever. Next morning he told the King, 'How could I take my ease at home, knowing all my friends in the army were sleeping rough under the stars at the Eastern front?' Uriah had spent the night with the King's servants, sleeping in the courtyard.

Annoyed, the King told Uriah that he would have to wait another day (and, by implication, another night), before he returned to the Eastern front.

That night David left nothing to chance. Uriah was putting duty before pleasure. The King needed some means to bring his military champion down to his own moral level. He chose to get him drunk.

But even drunk, Uriah the Hittite was the moral superior of Israel's King. He spent a second night in the courtyard.

When, the following morning, Uriah mounted his horse for the return journey to the front, he was handed a package of sealed orders. The sealed orders contained his own death warrant. The squalid one-night stand had to be covered up, apparently. And, apparently, the cover-up demanded Uriah's death. The spin strategy had not worked out; so David was about to use murder as his exit strategy.

[1] The story is found in 2 Samuel 11.

[2] 2 Samuel 23:34, 39.

[3] 2 Samuel 11:7, *Anchor Bible*.

2

Outrageous!

The sealed orders carried by Uriah went something like this:

'Dear Joab, Time for a suicide mission. Put Uriah where the fighting is fiercest. I want him dead. Your King, David.'

Until the Bathsheba affair, David had always been known for generosity of spirit and largeness of heart. But those sealed orders to Joab revealed a very different spirit, the worst. He had bypassed spiritual schizophrenia and gone directly to living without God in view, and done so with never a backward glance. He had turned his back on God and was behaving as if he did not exist.

As a young man, David had been called 'a man after God's own heart'.[1] At 50 he was appearing as a lust-crazed abuser of absolute power who would stop at nothing.

Much later, the King was told that his wicked actions had 'caused the *enemies* of God to blaspheme'. But how do you think Joab felt when he read those sealed orders, handed to him by Uriah? How do you think Joab felt towards his psalm-singing king?

Whatever Joab felt, it did not prevent his arranging the suicide mission. The siege of Amman took a new turn. A large contingent of the army, including Uriah, was ordered to attack right under the city walls. From there the Ammonite archers were able to pick the Israelite party off one by one. The casualty figures were high. Even Joab, normally more careless of human life than his king, was concerned about them. That concern and the hard-bitten cynicism that the King's sealed orders had induced were apparent in what Joab said to the messenger he sent to report to Jerusalem. It amounted to this: 'Oh yes, and if the King complains that the casualty figures are a bit high, add this, "Your servant Uriah the Hittite is dead." That'll fix him!'[2]

Beneath the walls of Amman, wives other than Bathsheba had lost their husbands; and parents, their sons.

Meanwhile, back at the palace?

David was taking it all in his stride. After a brief period of ritual mourning for Uriah, the King married Bathsheba.

Do we know what Bathsheba felt about all this?

Can we, as has been suggested, blame her for seduction-at-a-distance by taking a shower in the back yard?

Most Bible authorities agree that bathing in those days was invariably done, when it was done at all, in the back yard. A fragment of 2 Samuel 11:4 suggests that it was in the nature of a ritual bath that took place at the end of Bathsheba's menstruation. A word in verse 26 suggests that she really grieved for Uriah. That fact suggests that Bathsheba was emphatically not in the mood for her second marriage.

Did David care? It's doubtful. He was intent on the cover-up. And, if he had indeed cared, he managed to console himself with the thought that only one man knew that Uriah's death, together with the deaths of the others picked off by the Ammonite archers, was not down to the fortunes of war, and that that man was Joab.

The problem for those, like David, who behave in atheistic mode, is that God doesn't go anywhere. No matter how many people behave as if he isn't there, God assuredly *is* there. Hence the final sentence of the biblical story: *'But the thing David had done displeased the Lord.'*[3]

Of the ten commandments, it has been suggested, King David had broken five. The Lord had a lot to be displeased about. The betrayal of Uriah. The exploitation of Bathsheba. The adultery. Taking his ease while others fought his battles. Deliberate, premeditated, choreographed murder. The cynical abuse of power.

God does not take kindly to those things. Political leaders may think that they are above the law, but they are not above God's law. And God makes no exceptions. He holds them responsible for their actions. God is keeping score. He does not overlook ethnic cleansings, suicide missions, 'convenient' massacres (or inconvenient ones!).

God holds leaders responsible if they launch wars to improve their poll ratings, or to capture weapons of mass destruction that they know do not exist, or to safeguard oil revenues.

God holds to account all those leaders who abuse those they are meant to serve.

God is keeping score.

There has to be a judgement at the end of history, otherwise much of history would make no sense.

David had ordered his behaviour and his cover-up as if there were no God. But God had not gone anywhere.

And what was life like for King David – the prodigal king playing away from the Father's House?

David, when he was not behaving badly, was often writing poetry. Many of his poems have survived in the book of Psalms. Hence, unusually among Old Testament figures, we can know what David thought, as well as what David said. It would appear that God does not give up on the spiritually bi-polar.

It is likely that Psalm 32 was a poem written by David at this stage in his life. This is how he describes his experience before his decision to confess his sin to the Lord (verse 5).

When I kept silent
My bones wasted away
Through my groaning all day long.
For day and night
Your hand was heavy upon me;
My strength was sapped
As in the heat of summer. (Verses 3 and 4.)

There was a prodigal who was not enjoying the Far Country and decidedly missing the Father's House.

The joy had left David's life. The feel-good factor had evaporated. Only when he decided to make a clean breast of it and acknowledge his sin before the Lord did he find the 'hiding place', the 'guard' that had all along been waiting to enfold him in salvation and 'unfailing love' (verses 7 and 10).

It was at that point that David heard the parent voice of God,

'I will instruct you and teach you in the way you should go;
I will counsel you and watch over you.' (Verse 8.)

Only when David chose to be upfront and confess did he leave behind the days and nights of black-dog depression.

[1] 1 Samuel 13:14.
[2] See 2 Samuel 11:24.
[3] 2 Samuel 11:27.

3

Saving grace

It was then that Nathan came calling. Nathan: God's prophet.

Our best friends are the ones who love us enough to confront us. Nathan confronted the King. On behalf of God. On behalf of the nation David led. On behalf of *Justice*.

Nathan was used to presenting to David the facts about judicial cases; and used, too, to inviting his adjudication.

Nathan did so on that occasion. He told him of a miserly rich man with flocks and herds who, needing to feed a visitor, instead of killing one of his own animals, took and killed the one ewe lamb owned by a poor neighbour.

David all but exploded with anger and made this startling pronouncement to Nathan: 'The man must pay and the man must die!'

After, perhaps, a moment of silence, Nathan turned on David and said, unforgettably, *'You are the man!'*

The King was sent reeling. Before David could recover himself, Nathan went into some detail to explain the consequences of his sin in what would become the most dysfunctional of royal families.

I read the Bible through for the first time when I was 13. When I reached that story I really enjoyed Nathan's denunciation of the King. I enjoyed it further as Nathan told David exactly where he got off. I could relate to that.

When David responded, 'I have sinned against the Lord',[1] I thoroughly approved.

But I was totally unprepared for Nathan's reply: 'The Lord has taken away your sin. You are not going to die.'

'NO!' I yelled. Something was seriously wrong here. I wanted David to suffer, *really suffer*. 'The Lord has taken away your sin' struck entirely the wrong note as far as I was concerned. What was the problem? Was God fresh out of fire from Heaven? I wanted the King roasted on a spit over a good hot fire.

Almost in panic I looked back at the page and read, 'After Nathan had gone home . . .' – and then I shut the book. It was my intention never to open it again.

David had pronounced sentence on himself: 'The man must pay and the man must die!' and I wanted Nathan or God or both – or anyone – to carry out that sentence. My youthful feelings were outraged.

I went back to 2 Samuel 12 one last time to make sure I had not misread something. No. There it was. Disgusted, I closed the book.

I took the issue to the only Bible authority on hand, my mother. She told me that her father, my grandfather, had given up on the Bible when he'd read that King Solomon had a thousand wives and concubines. But, said Mother, at least Grandad had been disgusted with King Solomon. It appeared that *I* was disgusted with God! *Scandalised with God?*

When you had fallen off a horse my mother was the sort of person who believed that you should get on again immediately. Hence she urged me to open my Bible again before it got cold. 'You might find Psalm 51 helpful,' she said.

Her strategy worked, at first. I opened the Bible to Psalm 51 and began to read. 'A psalm of confession and repentance written by David following his encounter with Nathan,' my Bible said.

The sanctimonious early-teen tick that I was found the tone of the opening verses about right. But I found something else to be outraged about in verse 4: *'Against you, you only, have I sinned and done what is evil in your sight.'* It was addressed to God!

So what about Bathsheba? Hadn't the debauched King sinned

against the young woman whose body he had exploited? Hadn't he sinned, too, against her husband, his military champion Uriah? I thought of his returning to the front carrying the sealed orders that contained his own death warrant. Hadn't the whole sordid business been an outrage by a king against his people – *all of his people?* Shouldn't justice come into it somewhere?

There were two verdicts. The first, David's own: *'The man must pay and the man must die!'* The second, Nathan's: 'God forgives your sin. You will not die for it.'

I favoured the first!

'Against you, you only, have I sinned. . . .' What did that mean? Mother suggested that I consult my father's impressive set of Bible commentaries. That helped a bit. It said that David had not meant to imply that Uriah and Bathsheba had not been wronged. 'But all sin in its ultimate nature is sin against God,' it went on. It reminded me that Joseph had said to the seductive Mrs Potiphar, 'How . . . could I do such a wicked thing *and sin against God?*'[2]

Did that help? I wasn't quite sure.

I'd heard my father refer to C. H. Spurgeon as some great Bible authority. I scented down Spurgeon on the Psalms. There I read: 'The psalmist's sense of sin towards others rather tended to increase the force of his feeling of sin against God. . . . The penitent's heart was so filled with a sense of the wrong done to the Lord himself, that all other confession was swallowed up in a broken-hearted acknowledgement of offence against him *". . . in your sight".*'

That was when the electric light went 'ping'!

From the time he had seen Bathsheba in the shower to the time he encountered Nathan, David had behaved as if there were no God.

Nathan, among other things, reminded the King that he owed his life and position to God, and much else besides.

The King who had once been 'after God's own heart' had been deeply unhappy away from God's presence. Spiritual schizophrenia was more distressing than *de facto* atheism. He was mortified when the realisation struck that God had been around all along.

This is how Spurgeon concluded his explanation:

'David felt that his sin was committed in all its filthiness in God's presence. None but a child of God cares for the eye of God, but where there is grace in the soul it reflects a fearful guilt upon every act, when we remember that the God whom we offend was present when the trespass was committed. . . .'

The word of God through Nathan convicted David and turned him round. He no longer saw the glamour of the woman he stole, nor the innocence of the man he had murdered. Those were the secondary charges. Once they had been dealt with there remained only the outrage of the One who was outraged by every sin. The bottom line of the narrative of the David-Bathsbeba affair was: *'But the thing David had done displeased the Lord.'*[3]

Two things led to David's no-holds-barred, no-special-pleading, abject confession and repentance.

The first was his hunger for the presence of God and desire to be restored to his joyful status as God's friend.[4] The second was that he was floored by God's great grace when Nathan responded to his confession, 'The Lord has taken away your sin.'

After that, Nathan had gone home because his work was done.

David's work was not done. He spent whole nights prostrated before God on the ground in penitence and confession.

He poured out his soul.

Grace made the difference. It cured atheism and dispelled spiritual schizophrenia at a stroke.

When Saul had confessed, he had said, in effect, 'I have sinned; please preserve my reputation.'[5] David knew that his reputation was past saving. He knew spin was nothing. Truth was everything. His reputation with God was the only reputation that counted.

David approached God with empty hands. All he had to offer was the sin for which he needed divine forgiveness.

He knew that repentance involved forsaking sin as well as confessing it. Hence his plea for 'a pure heart' and 'a steadfast spirit'.[6]

One sentence David used hints that he understood, if only

distantly, how God's grace to a penitent sinner was possible:

'Cleanse me with hyssop, and I shall be clean.'[7]

The King was familiar with the fact that the Israelites, following the prescription in Leviticus, dipped hyssop in blood during the healing process. Even more importantly, he understood that hyssop branches were used to sprinkle the lambs' blood on the doors and the lintels of homes on Passover eve, recalling the Exodus.

Whether he fully grasped it or not, David was claiming cleansing through the sinless Son who would be born of his line – and whose death would be a substitute for his own.

God's unswerving commitment to justice and God's undying longing to redeem sinners met at the Cross.

Aged 13, I was scandalised and outraged by God's grace. And I closed my Bible.

But I opened it again. It has remained open ever since.

What has kept it open has been that I have continued to find God's grace both scandalous and outrageous.

[1] The story continues in 2 Samuel 12. This quote is from verse 13.
[2] Genesis 39:9.
[3] 2 Samuel 11:27.
[4] Psalm 51:11, 12.
[5] See 1 Samuel 15:30.
[6] Psalm 51:10.
[7] Psalm 51:7.

4

The lure of the Far Country

Prodigal is an astonishing word. There are a few words – like *extravagant* – that go some distance towards meaning the same thing, but run out of puff well short of the finish.

The best definition of prodigal is *overgenerous to the point of wastefulness*.

So who are the principal characters in Jesus' most famous story, and which one is the most prodigal?

There's the heartless scamp of a younger brother. There's the hard, alienated older brother. There's the overwhelmingly awesome Father who was not like any other father of whom the hearers of Jesus had ever heard.

And there was a fourth character. He's not mentioned. He's implied. The story does not make sense without him.

The starring role in Act One was taken by the heartless younger brother. The law entitled him to one third of his father's estate in one specific circumstance: when his father was dead. Not prepared to wait that long, he impatiently approached his father and said, 'I don't want you, but I want my share of your things; and I want it NOW!'

Talk about brass-necked, brazen-faced effrontery! What that boy said beat all previous records.

Put yourself in the shoes of that father. What would you have said and done? Had I been the father, there would have been considerable danger of the young scamp's exiting my property with the print of size 8 Hush Puppies on his fundament.

The boy made his demand in a way that meant that his father's life and all he had worked for meant nothing to him. He wanted his money, he wanted it then, and he wanted out.

That father absorbed the hurt to his heart and to his prestige, and set in motion plans to comply with the younger son's wishes. Whether by remortgaging or selling off land, he raised the equivalent of one-third of all his assets. He gave the capital to his younger son; and watched him ride off into the sunrise and towards a Far Country.

Act Two. The younger son, lost to his family, was frittering away a hard-earned fortune in the gambling and red-light joints of a distant city. For company he had the Hurray Henrys and Hurray Henriettas who always show up when there's a fortune to be squandered.

The underworld bosses who ran gambling and prostitution in the Far Country were as mean and greedy as such people are anywhere else. They made hay while the sun shone. And when it stopped shining? They were a lot richer.

The lost son, however, was out of loot. The rackets continued uninterrupted. The Hurray Henrys and Hurray Henriettas left town in search of another sucker. And life in that city went on.

The lost son discovered that the Far Country had no welfare system to care for out-of-loot losers. And further, that its policy towards lost sons and daughters was to pack them off to the pig farm.

No wages. No food. Nothing but pigs. The lost son was so famished he found himself salivating at the sight of pigswill. However, famine focuses the mind wonderfully, and he found himself recalling that even the day-labourers on his father's farm had 'food enough and to spare'. . . .

Act Three represents the crowning point of the saga. The beggarly, fresh-from-the-pig-farm lost son (if *fresh* is the word I want) struggled towards home, rehearsing the speech he would make to his father. While he was still a great distance from his home, he caught sight of a figure hastening towards him – his father, running. No Eastern father ever ran in a circumstance like that. He stood on his dignity. He would wait, impassive, until the returning wastrel struggled up the steps to the veranda – and then decide whether to recognise his existence or not. Given what he had done, 'not' was the more likely option. When the audience who heard Jesus say that 'the father ran', they were aware that he was not like any father they knew.

The father *ran*. Until the penniless prodigal saw his father's outstretched arms, he might have been alarmed. He blurted out the first part of his prepared speech: 'Father, I have sinned and am no longer worthy to be called your son. . . .'

Before the boy could continue – he had planned to say, 'Please take me on as a day-labourer' – the father engulfed him in a bear-like embrace, interrupting his flow of words with a series of commands, fired off towards his servants running behind him:

'Quick! Fetch shoes for his feet!'

Shoes meant the boy was free and family – not a day-labourer.

Then: 'Bring the ring for his finger.'

That indicated that he was being received as a son and heir – as if he had never left for the Far Country.

The father had not done: 'Bring the best robe and put it on him!'

The best robe in the house was the father's best robe. It had to be. He was giving it to a returning scamp who stank of the pig farm.

When Jesus brought his story to a close, a party to celebrate the return of the wastrel was in full swing and the father was saying, 'This my son was dead, and is alive again; was lost, and is found.'

Hollywood would have run the credits then.

But Jesus who told the story did not end there. . . . .

5

The welcoming Father

The father – running to meet the waster.

The father – embracing the squanderer.

The father – interrupting the scamp, before he could ask for a job, to accept him back as a son and heir.

Since *prodigal* means 'overgenerous to the point of wastefulness', who deserves that label?

The younger son's initial demand from his father had announced what sort of person he was. Since then he had stayed true to type. Even his decision at the pig farm had not been especially remarkable. He had 'come to his senses'. Starvation had focused his mind to the point where the most plausible survival strategy had been to make tracks for home.

From the time when he had raised the funds demanded by his younger son to the time when he threw a party in honour of his return, the father did wonderfully amazing, truly prodigal things.

The fact that the father ran to greet his son suggests that he had been looking and hoping for his return ever since he left.

At some point the penniless son became the penitent son. It was at that point that a change began in the character of the waster. It didn't happen at the pig farm. It happened in the father's embrace. It always does. Prodigal grace triumphs over prodigal sin in the Father's embrace. Lives begin to turn around then. This is why it is vital that returning wanderers meet the Father before they meet the older brother. . . .

When sin is forgiven, someone has to pay. When the returning waster was received as a son and heir someone had to bear the cost. That had to be the father and the older brother. Why the latter? What the waster had wasted was his one-third share of the family business. Of the estate, both the father and the older brother had to relinquish part of their wealth, thereby exhibiting prodigal grace to the one who had shown himself to be thoroughly undeserving.

The father was willing to pay. The older brother, most decidedly, was not.

The party arranged to celebrate the return of the younger brother was the sort of event you could hear at a considerable distance. It brought the older brother in from his work in the fields. He summoned a servant and demanded to be told what was afoot. He was told. 'The older brother became angry and refused to go in,' said Jesus, the narrator of the story. 'So his father went out and pleaded with him. . . .'

Jesus told three 'lost' stories. The Lost Sheep. The Lost Coin. The Lost Son.

Those stories were told at a point in his ministry when 'large crowds were travelling with Jesus'.[1] The crowds contained a disproportionate number of 'tax collectors and sinners'. Enough, in fact, to excite comment. The comment was made by Pharisees and lawyers, respectable people who wanted to put the hoi polloi in a different category from themselves. Looking down their noses, they said of Jesus, 'This man welcomes sinners and even eats with them!'[2]

It was that comment that led Jesus to tell his three 'lost' stories, one after the other.

The first featured a shepherd who owned a hundred sheep, one of which wandered away. The shepherd gave priority to the lost sheep, leaving the ninety-nine to go in search of it. Ignoring personal danger, the shepherd searched for the sheep until he found it. There was rejoicing and celebration when he was successful.

The second story featured a woman who saved up ten silver coins, but lost one. She took her lamp and turned the house upside down until she found the lost coin. Her neighbours rejoiced with her.

Jesus told those stories to establish a pattern. The Loss. The Search. The Celebration. Then he told the story of the lost son to address the mindset of the sanctimonious lawyers and Pharisees. In doing so he implicitly led his hearers to expect the same pattern, and to question why its central feature was absent.

In the third story, no one went to the Far Country in search of the waster. He had to bring himself home. Not only did his older brother not set out, but also he failed to welcome his sibling on his return, refusing point-blank to be part of the celebration.

The father heard that his older son was out in the yard. He left the celebration and went to find him. Almost ran, actually.

The father found him in a rage. For every 'notorious sinner' who returns and is received and restored, there are those who mutter behind their hands. But the older brother did not stop at that. At boiling point he began with *'This son of yours . . .'* The father replied, '*This your brother* was dead and has returned to life again! He was lost but now he is found.' Under those circumstances a celebration was *necessary*. The family had kept back resources for a special occasion. And, as far as the father was concerned, occasions did not come any more special.

The older brother received the invitation to join the party with contempt. Furious, he spat these words at this father: 'All these years I've slaved for you and done everything you asked of me. And in all that time you never even gave me a young goat for a feast with my friends. Yet, when *this son of yours* comes back again after squandering his money on prostitutes, you celebrate by killing the fattened calf!'[3]

The father responded: 'My son, you are always with me, and everything I have is yours.' And that was the literal truth. The two-thirds inheritance left behind after the younger brother took his one-third share belonged to the father during his lifetime. Beyond that, it belonged to the older brother. There is a sense, therefore, in which the older brother had been 'slaving' for himself, but a sense, too, in which, by restoring the younger brother as a son *and heir* to what remained of the estate, the father was expecting the older son to share his own prodigal grace towards the younger brother. But he didn't!

The younger brother was prodigal with material things. The father was supremely prodigal with his grace. But had the older son been prodigal?

As the first heir of *such a father*, he had had unlimited exposure to his all-gracious personality. But in a vital respect he had not accepted his father's grace, had not become gracious and, therefore, had not been driven to extend that grace to others.

The older brother had lived in close proximity to the father, but at a prodigious distance from the father's heart. First, by failing to go in search of his young, misguided brother; and, second, by failing to welcome him on his return, the older brother had been prodigal with the father's grace. He had not received it; therefore he could not radiate it.

Jesus told the three 'lost' stories of the fifteenth chapter of Luke's gospel because the Pharisees had said, 'This man receives sinners.' The Lost Sheep and the Lost Coin stories were told to establish a pattern: **1.** Something is lost. **2.** Someone goes in search of what is lost until it is found. **3.** There is a great celebration after the lost is found.

He told the third story to demonstrate the contrast between God's love towards the lost and the hostile alienation of the Pharisees (represented by the older brother).

Having established the 1, 2, 3 pattern in the Lost Sheep and Lost Coin stories, Jesus wanted his hearers to expect that the pattern would be repeated in the Lost Son story. The Lost Son story contained no search for the son who was lost. The one who had the responsibility for the search was the older brother. Not having accepted his father's grace, the older brother was not driven to carry that grace to his younger brother, either by searching for him or, when he returned, by welcoming him.

Apart from giving the Pharisees a much-needed object lesson, the story was also meant to encourage lost sons and lost daughters to enter the embrace of an all-gracious, all-welcoming Father.

[1] Luke 14:25.
[2] See Luke 15:2.
[3] See Luke 15:28-30, NLT.

6

The true Elder Brother

By casting a deeply flawed person as the older brother Jesus, the narrator, leaves us dissatisfied and longing for a true Elder Brother.

In the Lost Sheep story the shepherd took on the wolves and the wilderness hazards until he found and rescued the lost sheep.

In the Lost Coin story the woman took her lamp and searched in every nook and cranny until the lost was found.

But in the Lost Son story, who went to the Far Country in search, found the lost boy and restored him to his loving father? No one. The older brother was the only one who could have, but he failed even to enter the celebration when, by the boy's own initiative, the younger brother returned.

The bitter, alienated, ungracious character of the older brother makes us long for the true Elder Brother, who will share the prodigality of the Father. We long for the Elder Brother who is also the Good Shepherd who will leave the fold, trek to the Far Country and search every wilderness wadi and mountain cave until the lost is found. And the Good Shepherd, we may recall, 'lays down his life for the sheep'.[1]

When lost sons and daughters return to the Father's House – by whatever means they have come – the Father leaps up, runs, smothers them in an embrace; and all is not only forgiven, it is forgotten.

But the strategy of the Father goes even further than that. The

Father initiates the search for the lost. His Son, the true Elder Brother, who shares his prodigality and his life, leaves the comforts of home for the profoundly alien environment of the Far Country. There the Son, the Elder Brother, seeks out lost sons and daughters in the streets and sin joints, and he invites them home. Sharing the Father's character, the Son cannot cope with the absence from home of lost brothers and sisters any more than the Father can with lost sons and daughters.[2]

Forgiveness, redemption and restoration always come at a cost to the one who forgives, redeems and restores.

The lost son in the parable was unfortunate enough to have a Pharisee for an older brother. He had squandered one-third of his father's fortune. His older brother was not willing to share the two-thirds inheritance that remained with him. 'There was no way for the younger brother to return to the family unless the older brother bore the cost himself. Our true elder brother paid our debt, on the cross, in our place.'[3]

The true Elder Brother's death. The Father's embrace. They are connected.

When we see the Father, arms outstretched, running towards returning prodigals, our hearts are warmed.

When we see God's perfect Son – the true Elder Brother – with arms outstretched and nailed to the crossbeam, we see the cost of our redemption. Hearts are broken. When that happens – cue new birth and heavenly celebration. An outcast has returned to God's family.

The true Elder Brother became an outcast so that we outcasts might re-enter the family as heirs. The true Elder Brother took the blame so that we might be received as blameless. The true Elder Brother was stripped of his robe so that we might wear the best robe of his perfect righteousness. On the Cross he bore the cost of our folly, and paid the price.

The true Elder Brother is the Good Shepherd 'who gave his life for the sheep'. Jesus said, 'I am the gate for the sheep. . . ; whoever enters through me will be saved. . . . I have come that they might have life, and have it to the full.'[4] He continued, 'My sheep listen to my voice; I know them, and they follow me. I give them eternal life, and they shall never perish; no one can snatch them out of my hand. My Father, who has given them to me, is greater than all; no one can snatch them out of my Father's hand.'[5]

How prodigal is that?

The Father loves to lavish grace on the left-out, the used-up and the put-down.

The Father's love: limitless.

The Father's grace: measureless.

The Father's power: unbounded and infinite.

'While he was still a long way off, his father saw him and was filled with compassion for him; he ran to his son, threw his arms around him. . . .'[6]

When the Pharisees complained of Jesus, 'This man receives sinners,' they, unintentionally, expressed the core of the Christian Gospel and provided Jesus with an opportunity to tell the story that lays bare the very heart of the Father God. The starring role in the parable of the lost son is enacted by its narrator, the Son of God, who, with the Father, welcomes every repentant sinner into his Kingdom.

1 John 10:11.

2 John 3:16; Matthew 9:13; 11:19; Romans 5:8.

3 Timothy Keller, *The Prodigal God* (Hodder and Stoughton), page 85.

4 John 10:1-30. See especially verses 7-11.

5 John 10:27-29.

6 Luke 15:20.

7

The place of brokenness

His full name is Mephibosheth. Let's call him M.

Where M lived is easier to pronounce – *Lo Debar*. Lo Debar is a Far Country where everyone is out of loot and even the pig farm has closed down. But the most important thing about Lo Debar is that it is impossible to find. And that was why M lived there.

M was a king's grandson. But there had been a change of regime. When news of the outcome of a battle had arrived at court, there had been panic. In the ancient Middle East a change of dynasty was apt to mean the liquidation of every member of the outgoing royal family. In the confusion the defeated king's grandson, M, then aged 5, suffered an accident that left him permanently disabled.[1]

Every country has its 'Back of Beyond'. You know, just past the boondocks, and through the backwoods. In ancient Israel it was *Lo Debar*, 'the place of brokenness or barrenness'. The no-hopers lived in Lo Debar. But even a no-hoper could live in a shack of his own. You had to be a no-good no-hoper to live in *lodgings* in Lo Debar. But somehow M, the late king's grandson, found his way to that broken place lost in the barren hills and became a lodger. His grandfather, King Saul, and his father, Jonathan, were dead, and the best thing that could be said of M was that he was lost and that he preferred it that way.

M was seriously disabled. But his worst disability was his

lineage. Unaware that incoming King David had mourned the death of his father and grandfather, M lived in fear of his life. 'Keep a low profile' was his motto. That made him the lowest nobody in a community of nobodies. Who would be interested in a 'dead dog' like him?[2]

His life's ambition? To survive, unnoticed, lost to the world.

Twenty years or so into his reign, King David, in Jerusalem, had reached the high plateau of his reign. After having won a kingdom of 6,000 square miles, he then controlled an empire of ten times that size. From Damascus in the north to the Red Sea in the south. From the Great Sea in the west to the Persian Desert in the east. There was peace and plenty in the land. Not that M of Lo Debar, then 25, knew much about that.

Until, that is, one great and glorious day.

In his palace King David was in expansive mood, conscious of God's great grace. He asked: ' "Is there no one still left of the house of Saul to whom I can show God's kindness?" '[3] David could think of no better way of responding to God's limitless grace than by extending it to the household of his erstwhile enemy.

Ziba, still managing the late King Saul's estates, was summoned into the King's presence.

Did he know of any surviving descendants of King Saul?

Ziba mused.

The dynasty had died out. *Or had it?*

Ziba's response to the King could be paraphrased like this: 'A son of Jonathan still survives. But your Majesty will not want to know him. He's an eyesore, crippled in both feet. He lives in . . . er . . . [pronounced with disdain] *Lo Debar.* And, what's more, even there he lives as a lodger. . . . He's unfit for the King's presence and unworthy of the King's notice.'

Without hesitation, the King commanded M to be brought up from Lo Debar – and you may imagine his feelings when soldiers from the King's garrison came to collect him!

David's question had been, 'Is there anyone out there?' And his message had been, 'If there is, let him come.'

Notice the question the King did *not* ask: 'Is there anyone *deserving*? Anyone with a good *CV*?'

The question of grace is always the same: 'Is there *anybody* out there?' And the message of grace is always the same: 'If there is, let him come.'

Liberating grace is love that stoops to redeem – an unconditional, limitless love, that extends not only to those who do not deserve it but to those who can never hope to deserve it. And one more thing: Grace is not grace unless it's *gratis*. When the *question* of grace is asked – 'Is there anybody out there?' – there is always a streetwise Ziba around to dish the dirt, and to say, 'You don't want to know him/her. He/she comes from the place of brokenness, Lo Debar. The creature is a no-good no-hoper.'

But the King repeats: 'Come! For there is a road from Lo Debar to the King's table.' Most routes to the King's table begin at *Lo Debar* (the place of brokenness).

So M was brought to court[4] and welcomed by the King, 'for the sake of your father Jonathan'.

M from Lo Debar was accepted and given the status of the King's own son and promised a permanent place at the King's table. The King stoops in grace and accepts the repentant sinner as a son, for the sake of *his* Son. The sinner, crippled in both feet, is in no way able to make his own way to the Kingdom of God.

To the folks at Lo Debar the King says, 'Whoever wishes, let him come.' And when we come, saying, 'I'm lost – but, yes, I want to leave Lo Debar; I want to sit in the King's presence; for the sake of the King's Son,' the King offers a place at his royal table.

There are no no-hopers in Lo Debar, because everyone there has received the King's invitation and, outside of town, there's a signpost pointing to the palace.

[1] 2 Samuel 4:4.

[2] 2 Samuel 9:8.

[3] 2 Samuel 9:3.

[4] 2 Samuel 9:5-7.

8

Love is the proof

Jesus can mend only broken people. But he doesn't break them. Life does that. He receives them, mends them and gives them new life.

How do the prodigal sons and daughters from Lo Debar respond to the new life they have been given?

In a country in which evenings are warm but in which it is dark by 6pm, evening meals are apt to be long, leisured, outdoor affairs.

Comfortably off people built their houses so that they formed three sides of a square. The square might feature a fountain and, at many seasons of the year, would be the setting for the evening meal – under the stars and the light from blazing torches.

Tables tended to be U-shaped. The food was served from the centre of the U. The family and their guests reclined on the outside of the U. Typically, they would recline on their left arm, leaving the right hand free to scoop in the food and gesticulate in conversation.

Because the evening meal was as much about conversation as about food, the host would often invite a celebrity guest. If he was well known, some uninvited people would turn up from the local community, stand around and listen.

Before the invited guests settled on their couches, the host would greet them individually. The greeting involved three things. First, there was the 'kiss of peace'. Second, the guest would be invited to sit, be relieved of his rudimentary footwear; and his dirty feet would be bathed in cool water. Finally, the host would make provision for a dab of perfume to be placed on the forehead of his guest.

A servant, specially designated by the host, would perform the second and third acts of courtesy for him.

The onlookers from the community would not expect that treatment. However, not to perform those services for an invited guest – and especially for the celebrity guest – would indicate churlish discourtesy on the part of the host.

Jesus was from time to time the special guest at such a meal. Each of the four gospels carries an account of one meal which was gatecrashed by a woman who anointed Jesus.[1] Luke's account names Simon the Pharisee as the host.

Pharisees – 'separated ones' – were self-righteous and, often, hypocritical. That Jesus was a special guest at a Pharisee's home was a little surprising. Was Simon a seeker? Perhaps a closet admirer? Probably not. He neglected to extend any of the three common courtesies to Jesus. The atmosphere of discourtesy suggests that he may have invited Jesus as part of an entrapment strategy. Or he may have simply heard about the young Galilean and invited him to give him the 'once over'. Whatever the reason, when he addressed Jesus as 'teacher', he was almost certainly being patronising or sarcastic.

Pharisees wanted to impress God – and anyone else who might be watching – by their strict adherence to rules and rituals. Keeping a squeaky-clean exterior was all that mattered to them. By contrast, Jesus favoured a holistic approach that began at the heart of a person. He used the dinner at Simon's house to teach his core values.

The female who let herself in at Simon's back gate is described as 'a woman who had lived a sinful life' in that community.[2] The connection with Simon was that he had led her into that sinful life:

that back gate had been all too familiar to her in former times. But the reason she risked his wrath by gatecrashing that party was that she just *had* to see Jesus. On a previous occasion he had led her out of her sinful life. 'Whoever comes to me I will never drive away,' Jesus said. She had come, found acceptance and new life and was about to perform an outrageous act of thankfulness to show her love and gratitude to Jesus.

It is likely that the woman had a stay-in-the-shadows-until-the-right-time strategy; and, when the deed was done, to make a swift exit.

Three things worked against the success of her plan. First, hypocrites never miss a chance to be judgemental. Second, everybody has a sense of smell and she was planning to anoint Jesus with *pure nard*, the most pervasively aromatic perfume there was. It came all the way from Nepal (wedged in the eastern Himalayas) and was an extract from the rare plant called *Nardostachys jatamansi*. The third thing that worked against her was her emotional nature. . . .

John's gospel reports that the woman was carrying 'a pint of pure nard' in her flask and that it was worth 'a year's wages'.[3] That would be in the region of 300 denarii. She was not about to anoint Jesus with a small bottle of scent, *but with her entire life savings*. Jewish women carried a flask of cheap perfume attached by a string around their necks. In today's money, this woman carried £25,000 worth of the world's choicest substance.

The time came for her to make her move.

She walked out of the shadows to perform her outrageous act of gratitude.

When she reached the feet of Jesus, everything went wrong. An emotional dam burst within her. Was it something Jesus said? Or maybe the state of his feet and what that implied about Simon's hypocritical attitude?

Whatever it was, deep emotions overcame the woman. She wept copiously over the feet of Jesus. She so far abandoned her concern for public opinion that she loosened her hair – something a respectable woman would not have done – and used it to towel

Jesus' feet. She then proceeded to kiss them. In no time her alabaster flask was broken and the feet of Jesus were covered with its aromatic contents. *And she had everyone's attention!*

Hard-line Simon was thinking hard-line thoughts: 'If Jesus was a prophet he would know about this woman. . . .'

Jesus was in a position to publish an exposé that would have devastated and discredited Simon. But he didn't take the opportunity. He told Simon a story which only he and Simon understood. Simon needed rescuing from sin, too. Jesus can mend only broken people, *but he doesn't break them. Life does that.*

'Her many sins have been forgiven – for she loved much,' Jesus told Simon. But the point was this. The woman was not forgiven because she loved. The reverse was true. She loved because she was forgiven. And that was the whole point.

The gospel Jesus preached was 'good news to the poor'.[4] Why? *Because God's grace is free at the point of need.*

There are three outrageous things about this story. The outrageous rudeness of the host. The outrageous act of love by the woman. The outrageous grace of the Saviour.

Love is the only appropriate response to outrageous grace. Love is the proof of new life.

[1] Matthew 26:6-13; Mark 14:3-9; Luke 7:36-50; John 12:1-8. Opinions vary as to whether these are different accounts of the same event, or whether one of the accounts is of a separate occasion. Here we are favouring Luke's account, but taking some details from the other three.

[2] Luke 7:37.

[3] John 12:1-5.

[4] Luke 4:18.

9

A Lamb at Passover

Two gospel writers – Matthew and Mark – indicate that the occasion when the woman gatecrashed Simon's party was only two days before the crucifixion.[1]

That being the case, the meal the following evening was noteworthy too. It was the occasion of the Last Supper.

For that meal Jesus was no one's guest. He was with his disciples. They had rented an upstairs room. Leonardo da Vinci's sixteenth-century painting of that first-century event has Jesus and the disciples occupying one side of a rectangular table. Not impossible, but, again, the U-shaped *triclinium* would have been more common. However, rather than being seated at the table, Jesus and the disciples would have reclined on couches.

The Passover meal was a commemoration of Israel's deliverance from Egyptian slavery. On the 14th day of the month of Nisan every Israelite household had been told to slaughter a lamb, daub some of its blood on the doorframe of the house, and eat the meat. Death would be obliged to 'pass over' the homes on which the blood appeared, but would enter where there was no blood.

The deliverance of a whole people from bondage and death had been subsequently celebrated by the Hebrew people at the Feast of the Passover. By the time of Jesus – almost fifteen centuries after the Exodus – some three million people would converge on Jerusalem for the Passover.

The year when Jesus and his friends met in that upper chamber, the feast took on a much deeper significance. Jesus instituted a meal that represented a deliverance far greater than that from Egypt. It meant deliverance from sin. Again deliverance would come as a result of blood. The blood of Jesus, the Lamb of God.

The death of Jesus by crucifixion would take place the following day. Jesus knew that. Despite his many warnings, the disciples had no more than a sense of foreboding. Hence, while the sins of the world weighed heavily upon Jesus, the disciples were far from grasping the gravity of the occasion. So far, in fact, that the substance of their conversation as they approached the upper room was the me-for-the-top-job game politically minded people play.

'The evening meal was being served.'[2] There was an awkward pause. The disciples first looked down their noses at one another. Then, suddenly, no one could meet anyone else's gaze. All were acutely aware that no one had performed the duties of the host. The basic courtesies had been neglected, as Simon the Pharisee had neglected them the night before.

The most pressing – because the most practically *necessary* – of the courtesies related to the state of the people's feet.

As always, Jesus and his disciples had spent that day in rudimentary footwear, tramping on unpaved roads fouled by animals and ankle-deep in garbage. It was about hygiene. It was about comfort. It was about washing away the cares and detritus of the day. The host, had they had one, would have arranged for a servant or slave to undertake the foot-washing. But there was no host; there were no slaves; they were on their own in a rented room. Hence the awkwardness.

Who would take on the role of the slave and wash the feet of everyone else? The disciples had been discussing who was the greatest. No one was, therefore, about to rule himself out of the 'greatness' stakes by assuming the role of slave to the rest. A document dating from shortly after the time of Jesus indicates that *Jewish* slaves were not to be required to undertake foot-washing. It was too demeaning.

A wife might wash the feet of her husband, and children of their father – but these were acts of extreme devotion. In an emergency, disciples might wash the feet of their disciple-master. However, the emergency did not exist in which it was appropriate for the disciple-master to wash the feet of his disciples.

Nevertheless, it was Jesus who broke the awkward silence. 'He got up from the meal, took off his outer clothing, and wrapped a towel round his waist.'[3]

Some have suggested that a wider circle of Jesus' disciples, including women, were present. That Jesus was the only person present prepared to assume the role of a servant suggests to me that no women were there. There would have been no awkward silence had there been just one. She would have been in there with towels and bowls!

Peter, for one, could not believe his eyes when Jesus prepared himself to wash feet.

'Master, *you* wash *my* feet?'

Jesus replied, 'You don't understand what I'm doing now, but one day you will.'

That made Peter reply with an even more emphatic refusal to allow Jesus to proceed. The response of Jesus was: 'Unless I wash you, you have no part with me.'

Only with the 20:20 hindsight of the Cross can we understand Christ's reply to Peter – and, therefore, the full significance of what Jesus was doing.

It was not about hygiene and etiquette. It was about sin and salvation. It was about the love of which God alone is capable. It was about the love that took Jesus to Calvary.

As long as we imagine that we can get by without Christ's cleansing, we are not saved and we cannot be saved.

When Jesus finished washing feet and resumed his place at table, the disciples began to discover that that was the significance of the bread he broke and the wine he blessed.

Jesus was within hours of becoming the ultimate Passover Lamb. He would submit to slaughter – his body would be broken and his blood shed – to wash away human sin, including yours and mine.

The foundation truth of Christianity is deeply politically incorrect. It is that there is no way to Heaven from your house – or anyone else's – except via Calvary.

Calvary is the next stop from Lo Debar.

After AD31, Passover would never be the same again, but the essence of its message continued to be, 'I will pass over you when I see the blood.'

Since Jesus stooped in humility to serve us through his Cross, how much more should we be prepared to wash the feet of the lowest and meanest of his followers?

Those who, having been humbled, come to Christ for cleansing, become the raw material of the community of humble servants that is the Kingdom of God.

[1] Matthew 26:6-13; Mark 14:1-11. See especially Mark 14:1.

[2] See the account in John 13:1-9.

[3] John 13:4.

10

Men caught in hypocrisy

The cast of characters included a manky, half-dressed woman, a heaving herd of lawyers and professional churchmen, a few onlookers, and Jesus.

The setting was the outer temple compound, at that time a building site with plenty of loose masonry.

The story was of a woman caught in adultery, an angry mob of men caught in hypocrisy, Jesus, and a number of spectators.

The frightened woman, 'caught in the act'[1] and glowing with shame and humiliation, was thrust by the outraged Pharisees into the presence of Jesus. 'In the Law, Moses commanded us to stone such women. Now what do *you* say?' they demanded of Jesus.

What *did* he say? Very little; nothing at all, at first.

That was significant. Jesus was showing us what to do. Tread cautiously. Pause. Think. Pray. Jesus knew all things, but was not quick to rush into judgement.

What were his options? The outraged Pharisees expected him to tell the woman, 'Your sins are forgiven.' Had he done so, they would have accused him of being soft on God's Law, soft on sin. If – and this was his other option – Jesus had confirmed their recommendation of the death penalty, they would have exposed him to the Roman authorities who had a monopoly on death sentences. Further to that, had Jesus recommended that the woman be stoned, he would have lost the devotion of the ordinary people who loved him because he was merciful.

That was a no-win situation with a touch of the Catch-22s.

Either Jesus condoned adultery or he took on Rome and lost his popular support at the same time.

When Jesus stooped and began to write in the sand, the outraged churchmen may have thought he was ignoring them.

To us it might seem odd that Jesus wrote on the ground at all, but in the centuries before blackboards were invented teachers often did that. That Jesus did not do it on any other occasion suggests that what he was writing was very important. In fact, the standard verb 'wrote' (*graphein*, as in graffiti) was not used. The verb employed was more specific (*katagraphein*), 'wrote against'.[2] That is so suggestive of what Jesus wrote that several manuscripts, some commentaries and the classic life of Christ, *The Desire of Ages*, suggest that Jesus was writing down the sins of the woman's accusers.

It was a setup. The churchmen knew it: *they* had set it up.[3] Jesus wanted them to know that *he* knew it. At the beginning of John 8 they wanted to stone an adulteress. At the end of John 8[4] they wanted to stone Jesus. Indeed, Jesus was their target all along. The use that the lawyers and churchmen were making of the woman was wholly cynical: she was a pawn in a game of which she had no knowledge. The victim and the onlookers were the only ones in the cast of characters present who were unaware that the Pharisees were not nearly as righteous as they pretended to be.

Indeed, one of the reasons Jesus paused before responding to them was that he wanted to provide them with an opportunity to contemplate the truly abominable exercise in which they were engaged. Less hardened cynics than these might even have been brought to repentance.

The accusers were right in saying that circumstances existed in which the Law of Moses would have inflicted the death penalty on an adulteress. But in those circumstances the adulterer would have to die, too. Part of the game-plan was that the male in the liaison had been permitted to escape. Either that or he was, as some commentators suggest, among those expressing hypocritical moral outrage.

There was a second male, conspicuous by his absence from the scene: the woman's husband. Since he was required to bring an action against his adulterous wife, his absence could be significant. The role of witnesses, such as the Pharisees, was not to initiate the action. Circumstances did exist in which they could carry out the sentence. However, to be valid witnesses they should have 'neither connived in any way in the sin, nor been backward in trying to prevent it'.[5] *Those* 'outraged' persons did not qualify as witnesses!

To recap, then.

A bunch of hypocrites on a self-righteous high. A manky woman. The Saviour of the world writing in the sand.

Before an especially irate Pharisee, I see him writing 'sadist'. Beneath the next set of sandals in the semicircle I see him writing 'malicious'. Then 'arrogant'. After that 'lecher'. Then 'plotter' and 'abuser' and 'deceiver' and 'libertine' and 'gossip' and 'bully'. In front of the most 'smouldering' Pharisee, did he write 'adulterer'?

'When they kept on questioning him, [Jesus] straightened up and said to them, "If anyone of you is without sin, let him be the first to throw a stone at her." '[6]

To me, that seems like a risky strategy. Jesus was giving permission for the stoning to begin under certain valid moral conditions. These men had loose masonry in their hands. They were on a hypocritical high. It would have taken only one of them to use his masonry as a missile. . . .

Jesus took the risk because he takes Law seriously. The same finger that wrote in sand had written the Law in stone.

For the second time, Jesus 'stooped down and wrote on the ground'.[7]

The masonry was dropped, not thrown. 'One by one, with bowed heads and downcast eyes, they stole away, leaving their victim with the pitying Saviour.'[8]

Jesus straightened and asked the woman where her accusers were, 'Has no one condemned you?'

The woman was bewildered. She had heard the words of Jesus, 'Let the sinless one throw the first stone' as her death sentence.[9] Where were all her pious accusers?

She replied, 'No-one, sir,' in some confusion. ' *"Then neither do I condemn you,"* Jesus declared. *"Go now and leave your life of sin."* '[10]

That verse takes my breath away. If you want a definition of grace, check it out.

From the sinful lawyers and churchmen: contempt for the weak, erring woman. From the sinless Christ: pity and words of hope and new beginnings.

Jesus does not diminish the sinfulness of sin. To those who say, 'I was born this way' or 'It came about because of my upbringing', Jesus still says, 'Go now, and leave your life of sin.' Grace is not a synonym for leniency. There is no grace without discipleship.

Grace is pardon and power for the penitent.

To say the words 'Neither do I condemn you', Jesus had to go to Calvary. That is the place of pardon where new life begins.

[1] John 8:4.
[2] Check John 8:6 in the Greek New Testament. Some manuscripts add that Jesus wrote down 'the sins of each one of them'. J. N. Saunders and B. A. Mastin, *Black's New Testament Commentaries: John* (A & C Black), pages 464-465.
[3] John 8:6.
[4] John 8:59.
[5] Bruce Milne, *The Message of John* (IVP). See also *The Desire of Ages*, pages 460-462.
[6] John 8:7.
[7] John 8:8.
[8] *The Desire of Ages*, page 461.
[9] *The Desire of Ages*, page 462.
[10] John 8:11, italics supplied.

11

The Champion who fights our battles

There were two main men in the story. One of them was a giant. The point of the plot was to determine which.

The backdrop to the drama was the wide Valley of Elah. It was divided in two by a pebbly brook, the Hebrew name of which meant 'the Boundary of Blood'. And there was an army on each side.

If giants are measured only by height, then that distinction belonged to Goliath. At nine feet nine inches he was a big fellow. But he was also a cautious fellow. From his bronze helmet downwards, his body was encased in metal. His body armour weighed twelve stone! As if that was not enough, he had a man to carry a heavy head-to-toe battle-shield that would protect his body from the enemy's arrows.[1]

Behind Goliath ranged the armies of the Philistines. On the other side of the valley, beyond the Boundary of Blood, bivouacked the army of Israel under King Saul, himself by no means a titch. But Saul was not the second man in the story. His was a bit part. The second man was David the shepherd boy who had come to the front line to bring supplies for his brothers fighting in the Israelite army. David had travelled fifteen miles from his father's home at Bethlehem. He carried ten chunks of cheese, ten loaves and other food essentials. If Bethlehem had had a branch of William Hill's, the clever money would all have been on Goliath's

Philistines.

David, fresh faced and freckled, arrived at the Valley of Elah in time to see the armies moving into battle positions, and to see Goliath step out from the Philistine hordes to taunt the Israelites as he had been doing for forty days already.

That's the form with giants. The giants that oppress us – fear, worry and the rest – don't just turn up once, deliver their menaces, rattle their sabres and leave. They do it day after day, trying to intimidate and wear us down by persistent pressure. King Saul was clever enough not to adventure the Israelite forces in conflict with utterly overwhelming odds. A 'let's-give-up-and-go-home' mentality afflicted Saul's soldiers.

First David dropped off his supplies with the quartermaster and greeted his brothers. By then he had heard the precise terms of Goliath's challenge. 'Why bother using your whole army? Pick your best fighter and pit him against me. If he gets the upper hand and kills me [fat chance], the Philistines will all become your slaves. But if I get the upper hand and kill him, you'll all become our slaves and serve us. . . . Give me a man. Let us fight it out together!'[2]

Goliath thought: Look at me! Nearly ten feet tall! And all that armour!

King Saul thought: It's been going on for forty days. If we survive, it will be through caution. Let's keep our heads down.

Young David thought: 'Who is this uncircumcised Philistine that he should defy the armies of the living God?'

Goliath's challenge boomed out. David saw a *frisson* of fear fizz through the Israelite lines; and sensed how fear in the face of bullies makes cowards of us all. And David was stung. The giant was cursing the God of Israel. No one talks that way about God! No one! So why was everyone taking cover?

A point of principle was involved. God was being insulted. And, to the evident embarrassment of his brothers, David began to share his clear-cut perceptions of what was going on. He told King Saul, ' "Let no one lose heart on account of this Philistine; your servant will go and fight him." '

God was a living reality to shepherd boy David. That had come about through prayer, meditation and the study of God's purposes. In the hills above Bethlehem David had acquired a fixed sense of the presence of God. And it gave him no end of power.

David's brothers were part of the defeatist mindset. They probably resented the fact that the runt of the litter was setting the pace. The freckle-faced youngster didn't get it, did he? He hadn't grasped the facts, had he? They told him: 'You're a spectator. Go back to the stands.'

David chose *not* to use his energy punching his brothers' lights out. The real enemy was Goliath. Right?

David's brothers, like King Saul, were impressed by the outward appearance of the giant. David was, in effect, saying, 'What giant? God is the only giant in my life! God is all powerful and can't lose.'

King Saul urged David at least to wear the King's armour. David refused. It was not just that Saul was 48L and David, 36R. It was that, in David's take on things, God eclipsed the 'giant'. David would be victorious. But the victory would not be won by the Lord *and* Saul's armour, but the Lord alone. That was the recipe for salvation, too. *The Lord plus someone willing to trust him.*

All David picked up was five smooth stones from the stream bed. His only help came from the Boundary of Blood. God entrusts us with our moment in history and invites us to trust him. He can empower us to do battle with giants.

Two armies, one on either side of the valley. Every eye was suddenly attracted to the slight young figure as, staff in hand, David emerged from the ranks of Israel and descended the slope. He picked up the five smooth stones and placed them in his shepherd's bag. By then he appeared so small he was almost invisible to either army.

Goliath felt affronted. He roundly cursed David and threatened that his blood would colour the mountain grass while his unburied body would provide a feast for the wild things. David responded: ' "You come out against me with sword and spear and javelin, but I come against you in the name of the Lord Almighty, the God of the armies of Israel, whom you have defied." ' When we become totally identified by faith with the name of God, that name becomes a strong tower, a refuge, a battle cry, and the secret of victory.

The battle is the Lord's, David was thinking.

It was and it is.

But what about 'the giant'?

Goliath was a threat that never materialised. All shout and bluster. When David looked, he was dead. And the only giant on the scene was God.

We *do* face giants, of course: stress, sin, sorrow, guilt, death and judgement. And fundamental to all is the sin giant. It seeks to control and intimidate us 24/7 – and ultimately to destroy us.

Because the effects of this giant's influence are so destructive, we need the most radical solution ever devised.

The solution comes from the Boundary of Blood.

To slay Goliath, David had to pass from one camp to the other – across the Boundary of Blood. That was the source, under God, of the victory.

While the Israelite army cowered, David approached Goliath. The weak overcame the strong. From the Israelite camp there was a shout of victory.

Goliath had said, 'Give me a champion and I will fight him.' Everything had depended upon that champion.

It did and it does.

We trust in the Champion in order to be part of the victory.

That great Chinese Christian Watchman Nee once wrote, 'Our deliverance from sin is based, not on what we can do, nor even on what God is going to do for us, but on what *he has already done for us in Christ our Champion*. When that fact dawns upon us and we rest back upon it, then we have found the secret of the victorious life.'

[1] The full story is in 1 Samuel 17.

[2] 1 Samuel 17:8-10, MGE.

12

Zero to hero. Then down-down-down!

David's was a zero-to-hero story.

His rise began when his father called him from tending sheep to be a late entry in Samuel's king-selection process. Only a freckle-faced lad, David had become a friend of God in the solitude of the Bethlehem hills. Hence God chose him above all the others; and Samuel, who was to be his mentor, anointed him.

David's first royal appointment was as a court musician. But his victory over Goliath catapulted him to stardom. Overnight he became the army's champion, he even led it to victory over the Philistines.[1] Subsequently he married King Saul's daughter Michal and became soul mate of her brother Jonathan.

Everyone loved him. People even wrote songs about him.

It all got too much for King Saul, who had issues with paranoia.

That was when David began to learn about failure. One by one all the 'props' that supported his life were knocked away:

• Through Saul's jealousy, David lost his position at court and in the army – and therefore his status and security.

• Initially, Michal made common cause with her husband.[2] Having facilitated David's flight, she then became vulnerable to her father's devious plans. As a result, David found that he had lost his wife.

• David fled to his mentor Samuel. Saul discovered where he was. Three unsuccessful attempts were made by Saul's army to capture David. It became necessary for him to escape and move on in search of another protector. Shortly afterwards, Samuel died and David lost his wise counsellor.

• David's friendship with Jonathan, Saul's son, was rock solid through it all. There had been an oath sworn between the two friends. But political pressures must have driven them apart, geographically at least.[3] David had, in effect, lost his closest friend.

• All David had at that point was himself, his self-respect. But he lost that, too. He fled to Gath and offered his services to Philistine King Achish. To save his skin, David convinced himself that he had to feign lunacy. Achish asked his servants, 'Am I short of madmen that you bring this one to plague me?'[4]

All the props had gone.

And David was still running.

The zero-to-hero story was knocked back to zero. When David escaped Philistia, we are into minus quantities.

What followed was the episode in the Cave of Adullam. David lost the 20:20 spiritual vision. John Ortberg writes: 'The cave named Failure . . . [is] where you end up when your props, supports and crutches get stripped away. . . . Nobody plans on ending up in the cave, but sooner or later everybody logs some time there. . . . The cave is where God does some of his best work in moulding and shaping human lives.'[5]

When we're down from hero to zero and into minus quantities – all but subsumed beneath problems and difficulties – we are learning lessons we would never learn otherwise. Spiritual growth has been turned to fast-forward. And that can feel like spiritual chemotherapy. God did not send David into ten years of cave-and-wilderness experience. Life did that. At times he thought of himself as a loser, a failure. By the time he was through he knew that all along he had been a *learner*.

A person who sees himself as a loser is apt to behave like one and to attract the company of other losers. In the Cave of Adullam 'all who were down on their luck came around – losers and vagrants and misfits of all sorts. David became their leader. There were about four hundred in all.'[6]

Can you imagine that? Four hundred whingers, whiners, fretters and fussers?

Try again – but on a larger scale. Make allowance for the fact that they all brought their wives and families!

Because they all thought they were losers and not learners, they went around raiding other settlements.

That was David at rock bottom.

Some years into that failure phase David's community moved to Ziklag. One day when he and the four hundred were away on a foraging expedition, the Amalekites swept in, captured all the women and children and burned Ziklag and everything in it.[7]

When the raiding party returned, it was crunch time for David. 'David and his men wept aloud until they had no strength left to weep.'[8]

Then it got worse. The mood of the men turned ugly. The four hundred started to play the blame game. It had to be somebody's fault, right? When David overheard the men discuss the idea of stoning him to death, he felt totally vulnerable and without resources. It was the end of the line. Even the friendship of the whingers and the whiners had gone. How broke can you be?

It was then that David realised that he had one more Resource. 'David found strength in the Lord his God.'[9]

Only one Resource was left. And David discovered that that Resource was more than enough.

David had reached the end of his tether and discovered the fundamental crisis principle of Scripture. God's grace is sufficient for all emergencies. God's strength is maximised in times of our greatest weakness and vulnerability.[10]

That discovery made David abandon 'loser' for 'learner' status. Among the first things God taught him was how to recover the wives and children.

David found a fragment of faith, but God can work with even that. He presented his failure to God.

'Props' and 'supports' can become a substitute for God. They can focus our minds on the horizontal instead of the vertical. Once David refocused his life on the vertical, his failures fell into perspective. After that there was no way but upwards.

One really great Christian preacher of the Great Awakening wrote of 'a tough fibrous root that is all that is evil within us'. We cannot take that root to God's Kingdom. It cannot remain untackled. God works with us in the cave-and-wilderness phases of our lives to enable us to wrench it out.

It is in that phase that our learning curve is steepest. Jesus did time in the cave. There came a time when the crowds 'walked no more with him' and then the time when they 'all forsook him and fled'. Following the crucifixion, the disciples were saying, 'We had hoped that he was the one who was going to redeem Israel. . . .'[11] Notice *had hoped*.

Hoped, but hoped no longer.

To the naked eye it all looked as if it had ended in failure.

They had put Christ's body in a manmade 'cave'. They'd placed a mighty stone in place and put a seal upon it. Soldiers had been left to guard it.

But armies of millions with weapons of mass destruction could not have kept Christ in the grave.

The person to whom the disciples spoke their words of discouragement – 'we *had hoped* that he was the one . . .' – was The Risen Christ.

[1] The story is in 1 Samuel 18, 19. See especially 19:8.

[2] 1 Samuel 18:20, 21.

[3] 1 Samuel 20:42.

[4] 1 Samuel 21:11-16, NEB.

[5] John Ortberg, *If You Want to Walk on Water You've Got to Get Out of the Boat* (Zondervan), pages 138, 139.

[6] 1 Samuel 22:2, MGE.

[7] 1 Samuel 30:1-6.

[8] Verse 4.

[9] Verse 6.

[10] See 2 Corinthians 12:9.

[11] Luke 24:21.

13

Making sure the connection is ***alive***

Lessons are learned in the Cave called Failure. Lessons of grace.

But our first priority as we move from loser to learner status is to make sure that our vertical connection is *live* – and in regular use.

The important thing about Jesus is not just that he was and will be again – *but that he is.*

It is not just that he came and will come again – *but that he comes.*

Jesus comes to us in our prayer times and in our quiet times when we immerse ourselves in his Word (especially in the four gospels).

Ancient scholars used to debate whether Jesus was really present in the bread and wine of the holy communion, or whether they were 'just symbolic'. They missed the point about the communion service and every other form of worship. Jesus comes to us – is present with us – whenever we connect with him through worship, prayer and Bible study. His presence is there, with us.

G. K. Chesterton, author of the Father Brown stories, said, 'People have not tried Christianity and found it wanting. They have found it difficult and not tried it.'

Try worship. Try prayer. Try the Word. And keep trying until the connection – *and it will happen* – becomes live!

Adventure, and you will soon discover that you are adventuring with God.

That's how it worked for the people of Israel. And it led to the nation's bright and most blissful dawn.

What a dawn that was!

It had been a long time coming.

It came at the end of more than four centuries of slavery.

When slavery had begun, the Israelites had been one big extended family with twelve branches. The conditions of slavery notwithstanding, their numbers had grown exponentially.

Egyptian measures to reduce the Hebrew birth rate had, if anything, been counterproductive. Some experts believe that two million Hebrews took part in the exodus that followed the first Passover.

They did what was asked of them in the matter of the lamb's blood. While the Egyptians wailed, the Hebrews packed. Came the dawn and they were facing east and moving out. The sweet smell of freedom was in the air. Their departure was unhindered. At that stage the Egyptians were glad to see the back of them. It was a heady moment they would never forget.

The logistics of mass catering troubled few, if any; nor did any sanitation or medical challenges they were likely to face. Freedom and faith were everything as they made steady progress eastwards. Refreshment came from the wells of grace. Leadership came from an 80-year-old shepherd who followed a pillar of cloud.

Two million adults, thousands of children, with flocks and herds and carts and I don't know what else again – marching due east.

Then, suddenly it seemed, the Red Sea was ahead of them. And behind them was the 600-chariot mechanised army of a pharaoh who'd changed his mind and who was very, very angry.

Expecting slaughter on an industrial scale, they were eager for someone to blame. So who precisely had got them into that mess in the first place?

They were in the classic no-way-to-win situation. To the east: the Red Sea. To the north: Egyptian fortresses. To the south: hundreds of miles of blazing desert. To the west: an Egyptian army of rumbling chariots that were bristling with the spears of men who believed they had every reason to be angry and every excuse for excess.

So who, precisely, *had* got them into that situation?

In the opening verses of Exodus 14 it is clear that God had all but provided them with the co-ordinates of the Red Sea camp. And they were the co-ordinates of a no-way-of-escape ambush.

Is that what God does? Lead us into crises so he can teach us a thing or three?

Had God set up the ambush?

Between the freed slaves and the sea was Moses. Moses was trying to make himself heard. Check Exodus 14:13 for the orders God told him to give. There were three: • Don't be afraid. • Stand firm. • Watch God work.

Before the night of the exodus, the Israelites had never been outside Egypt. With a pillar of cloud by day and fire by night, they had never had to make a decision for themselves. Yes, God was putting them on the spot. But in doing that he was, in effect, saying, This is my crisis, not yours. Just watch me work.

Faith was being tested. The Israelites had received God's grace, and were being given an opportunity to *grow in grace*. People who had been slaves and had become servants were now being invited to become disciples.

Between the Israelites and the deep Red Sea, Moses was standing and saying, 'Stand still! Stop striving! God *will* come through!'

Moses had known God well enough and for long enough to trust him. He had served a forty-year apprenticeship for this moment. The Israelites had not, and panicked.

Moses had allowed God to conquer his fears. He had learned to wait patiently for God's timing.

The ambush by the Red Sea was not for the Israelites; it was for their enemies. But God used the crisis which had 'come to pass' to teach the Israelites three vital lessons:

• 'Don't be afraid.' Homespun philosophy says, 'God helps those who help themselves.' That is opposite to the truth. God helps the helpless who cry, 'Help me!'

• 'Stand firm.' Lessons can be learned in a crisis that cannot be learned anywhere else. It takes a crisis to break lifetime habits. When you're surrounded, the only way to look is up.

• 'Watch God work.' The biggest, most mechanised army of the world's only superpower was bearing down on the unarmed men, women and children of the Israelites. Expecting slaughter, they panicked.

Thankfully, however, before they gave way to their fears, they heard the threefold injunction of Moses. And, to give them their due, they heeded it. Had they acted on their panic they would have run into the sharp spears of the enemy.

As it was, they stood, then obeyed the command to march towards the sea. Moses raised his staff. The pillar of cloud before them became, at nightfall, the pillar of fire that kept the Egyptians at bay behind them. The wind blew. At dawn an impassable riverbed swamp had become a dry highway to freedom.[1]

They watched God work. *That* was an even more glorious dawn.

Yes, God permits tough times to get our attention. But he doesn't bring the tough times on. Yes, having got our attention, God uses the opportunity to deal with our issues.[2]

When our backs are against the wall, God is saying, 'Be still and know that I AM,' and WHO I am.[3]

What I should like to know is how in a crisis like that *Moses* had enough faith to stay calm, give God's orders and follow them through. . . .

[1] Read the full story in Exodus 14. This is a summary of verses 15-31.

[2] *Christ's Object Lessons*, page 177. See John 19:10, 11 and Romans 8:26-28.

[3] Psalm 46:10.

14

The making of a hero

When Moses led the Israelites from Egypt he was aged 80.

To prepare Moses to command a nation caught in crisis and prone to panic had taken God forty years.

It was far from on-the-job training; though it did take place in the theatre of operations where God with Moses would later build a ramshackle two-million-strong rabble into a nation.

It was not theoretical leadership training; though God did build on the knowledge of the law and logistics, mathematics and strategy, language and literature Moses had acquired in his years as a trainee pharaoh.

David was not ready for kingship when Samuel anointed him. He needed to be taught to depend on God during his cave-and-wilderness years.

Joseph was marked out for a leadership role when he was in his teens, but he was far from ready. Even his doting father found his self-centredness exasperating.[1] God used the tough stuff of Joseph's life to hone his skills, smooth his sharp edges and focus his vision.

The fact that God took *forty* years to prepare Moses to lead a slave race to freedom and forge a nation in an inhospitable desert reflected the scale of the job and the number of issues that needed to be tackled.

It is possible that Moses had grown up with the idea that one day he would be the man to liberate his enslaved people, the Hebrews. Centuries later, before the Sanhedrin, Stephen would imply that Moses' murder of the Egyptian overseer was meant to jumpstart the liberation movement: 'Moses thought that his own people would realise that God was using him to rescue them, but they did not.'[2]

Murder had not been in God's plan. It happened because at 40 the political instincts and/or anger of Moses had got the better of him. Moses had lost his vertical hold. That's why the murder happened. And that was one reason why Moses required a long course in God's university of hard knocks.

God's university had little to do with academia. Pharaoh's daughter had groomed Moses for Pharaoh's job. But God's grooming was to take a different form. He was looking for different results. The upshot of Moses' Egyptian education was the political initiative of killing the Egyptian. But the following morning found Moses jumpstarting a top-of-the-range camel and taking the shortest route to the nearest frontier.

Moses' flight took him to Midian where the trainee pharaoh became a trainee shepherd. God used Moses' forty years of caring for sheep in the bleak wilderness to teach him the lesson of Psalm 46:10. 'Be still. Stop striving. Know that I am God, above political stratagems. My purposes cannot be jumpstarted. Take a long loving look at your High God. Wait for his timing.'[3]

'The Lord permits trials in order that we may be cleansed from earthliness, from selfishness, from harsh, unchristlike traits of character. He suffers the deep waters of affliction to go over our souls in order that we may know him and Jesus Christ whom he has sent, in order that we may have deep heart longings to be cleansed from defilement, and may come forth from the trial purer, holier and happier.'[4]

On the day Moses murdered the Egyptian oppressor, far from initiating the liberation process, he set it back forty years.

God had his own methods and his own time-schema. Priority one was for Moses to renew his vertical hold.

To a trainee pharaoh, looking after Jethro's sheep in the back of beyond must have looked like failure. But Moses had to learn how to handle failure. Failure teaches us humility. Humility prompts a teachable spirit. A teachable spirit puts us into learning mode. Moses had to learn that you do not connive your way to leadership in God's enterprise. Nor do you fume and fret. You wait for God's timing.

God's leadership candidates are usually aghast at their own selection. At the age of 40 Moses was in a mood to get up, get active and get at 'em. After forty years in solitude and discomfort, losing his pride and ambition, Moses was rather less sure of himself.

There must have been days, weeks and months of the forty-year forward-to-maturity period when Moses wondered what God was doing. Towards the end of his life, in the Song of Moses, he could in retrospect see that God had led him every step of the way. In the 'desert land . . . in a barren and howling waste' God had 'shielded', 'cared for' and 'guarded' him.[5]

By the time God spoke out of a burning bush to invite Moses to lead the Exodus, his response was along the lines of: *'Why? What? Me?'*

Servant leaders are the only leaders God takes seriously. The Church is the Body of Christ. This being the case, there can be no lust for recognition, no celebrity culture.

In the desert, Moses, having broken himself, was being rebuilt by God. Having been ruined, he was being refined. God needed time, solitude and discomfort to deal with Moses' pride, fear and bitterness. That required a wilderness, not a five-star hotel in Sharm el Sheikh. There was no 'fast track' in God's desert school.

There, one day was apt to merge into another and one year seemed pretty much like the year that preceded it. Moses must have wondered, and wondered often, whether there was *any* purpose in those endless years of isolation.

But at some level we all have a choice to make of how we relate to life's discipline. The pain, or whatever the discipline is, can make us bitter or it can make us better. It can make us into losers or learners. The first step in relating to it is to put our hands in the hand of God. God is Lord also of the desert places of our lives.

When we're having an easy time of it we say, 'God is blessing me.' But God may equally be blessing when times are hard. The challenge is to invite God into whatever situation we find ourselves – to transform it. God is Lord, also, of the tough terrain. It is in those circumstances that we 'grow in the grace and knowledge of our Lord and Saviour Jesus Christ'.[6]

God wants learners, not losers. And what we learn in our tough times is how to deal with our dark side. God allows us our caves and our deserts so that pew-sitting consumers of religion can become disciples of Christ. Christianity must do far more than *enhance* life. It must transform it.

God doesn't use microwave methods, mega results in minutes. That reflects the fact that most of the time he has to work with sinful human beings. Why? There are no other kinds. And sinful human beings make haste slowly. And learn *very* slowly, and unlearn more slowly still.

Paul says that God puts his priceless treasure into 'a common earthenware jar'.[7] But, at the point when the priceless treasure is poured in, the earthenware jar may not yet have been fired up in the kiln or shaped by the potter. The firing up, and the shaping – that fit us for service – may involve some problems, pressures. But never despair. Paul says, 'We are persecuted, but we never have to stand it alone: we may be knocked down but we are never knocked out!'[8]

Through schools of adversity Abram, who lied to save his own skin, became Abraham, the friend of God. Rahab of the red-light quarter became Rahab of the Hebrews 11 'Hall of Faith', an ancestress of Jesus. John Mark, who let Paul down so spectacularly, became John Mark the author of the gospel and the man Paul most wanted with him in his final imprisonment.[9] Peter, who denied Christ three times, received a new commission three times after the resurrection. And Moses the murderer met the Lord of the second chance in the desert, and was recommissioned to lead God's people in a forty-year journey from slavery to the Promised Land.

Wherever you are at the moment, God says, 'Don't panic. I am with you. There's no need to fear for I'm your God. I'll give you strength. I'll help you. I'll hold you steady; keep a firm grip on you.'[10]

At whatever stage you are in your growth, two principles hold true:

His grace *is* sufficient for you.

His strength *is* maximised when your need is greatest.

[1] Genesis 37:2-11.

[2] Acts 7:25.

[3] Amplified from MGE.

[4] *Christ's Object Lessons*, page 175.

[5] Deuteronomy 32:10-12.

[6] 2 Peter 3:18.

[7] 2 Corinthians 4:7, Phillips.

[8] Verse 9, Phillips.

[9] 2 Timothy 4:11.

[10] See Isaiah 41:10, MGE.

15

Grace like a river

Luther compared the human heart to a cowshed at the end of winter. 'What can we do with all that filth?'

This was his prescription for the stinking cow byre. 'Turn the Elbe into it. [In place of Elbe read Trent or Severn, if it helps.] The flood will sweep away all the pollution. Not my own efforts, but the influx of that pardoning, cleansing grace which is in Christ, will wash away the accumulations of the years.'

That's grace like a river: the free, unexpected love of God to and through the undeserving. The grace that, while we are sinners and enemies, treats us like family members and heirs.

But that is not all there is about grace.

Grace is not just grace in the **function**: like a mighty river washing away uncleanness. Grace is grace in the **presentation**.

Grace is **message**. Grace is also **behaviour**.

For the last half of the nineteenth century the British scene was dominated by two great political rivals: Gladstone and Disraeli. An attractive woman sat next to each man at dinner on consecutive evenings. When asked to compare her experience of the two men, she replied thoughtfully, 'When I left the dining room after sitting with Mr Gladstone, I thought he was the cleverest man in England, but after sitting next to Mr Disraeli, I thought I was the cleverest woman.'

Gladstone was always 'on message'. But, on that occasion at

least, Disraeli was the one whose behaviour was gracious.

The grace of Jesus was not just in what he said, but in how he said it. Yes, he was in the business of making cowsheds end up smelling of roses. But he never lost sight of the fact that what he was really dealing with was *people*. Beneath and around the cowshed condition of the person was – *the human being*. A sensitive, vulnerable, easily distressed individual, who required rescue and was in search of the welcoming warmth of the Father's House.

To reach the woman with the cowshed experience, Jesus walked through enemy territory. A mile out of Sychar, a town which has its own water source, the main road forks. At the fork is Jacob's ancient well. It is a hundred feet deep. Jacob found no spring there, but had to dig until he reached the water table. Hence the water in that well was not what the Jews called 'living' (that is, running) water. It was water percolated through the subsoil. The well survived to the time of Jesus – and survives to the present day – because it was Jacob's well, not because it was a good well.

Jesus arrived in the heat of midday and was parched dry but did not possess a traveller's leathern bucket. The woman had walked from Sychar in the midday heat to the out-of-town well because she was a social outcast and believed that, by doing so, she could avoid all human contact. Too late she realised she had a Jewish rabbi for company and that, in addition to her five-weddings-and-a-relationship background, she was separated from him by five centuries of hostile history. In addition, she would have expected him to turn away from her, purely because she was a woman.

The Sychar woman was in for a surprise because the Nazareth Stranger was inhibited by neither racial nor gender prejudice.

Notice what Jesus did. He did not start in on the cow-byre aspect of things. His initial approach indicated his own vulnerability: 'Will you give me a drink?' For one of the few times in her life she found someone with kindness in his eyes; not critical superiority, not even *tolerant* superiority.

She began to open her heart. *She* reminded *him* of the ethnic, gender and historical baggage they should both be carrying.

Jesus responded, 'If you knew the gift of God and who it is that asks you for a drink, you would have asked him and he would have given you living water.'

The woman pointed out that Jesus had no bucket, that the well was deep and, further to that, if 'living water' was to be on offer, did he think he could do better than 'our father Jacob'?

That was Jesus' opportunity for a big put-down. Jews were outraged by the Samaritan claim to be descended from Jacob.

In place of a put-down, Jesus replied: 'Everyone who drinks this water will be thirsty again, but whoever drinks the water I give him will never thirst.'

What was on offer was the new life, the great river of living water that can wash away all sin and uncleanness and bring with it new life.

A Jew would have understood Jesus' words. **Isaiah** had spoken of drawing water from the wells of salvation. The **psalmist** had spoken of his soul being thirsty for the living God. **Isaiah** had said that the only qualification for receiving an outpouring of living water *gratis* was thirst. **Zechariah** had spoken of a new fountain that would spring up in Jerusalem to wash away all sin and uncleanness.[1]

But the Samaritan woman was the victim of a truncated Bible (the Samaritans accepted only the first five books). Hence she responded to Jesus with a jest: 'Sir, give me this water so that I won't have to keep coming to this well!'

It was time to be direct: 'Go. Fetch your husband. . . .' The woman stiffened and went white as if she had seen a spectre. She had. The spectre of her past and her present. The cowshed had been identified, *but only after the river of living water had been offered*. The announcement of the cure had preceded the diagnosis.

By dissolving every barrier that separated the Samaritan from the source of her salvation, Jesus had made it clear that the river of living water is a mighty, unstoppable current that cleanses, renews, revives to the point at which even the cowshed itself can become 'a spring of water welling up to eternal life'.

Jesus introduced himself as the Messiah. As the disciples came along, the woman was rushing back to town, the first missionary to Samaria.

What had made the difference? The *message* of grace? More than that. It was the *personification* of grace.

How often do we hamper the message of grace by our failure to personify it?

Jeremiah[2] complained that the people had forsaken the fountain of living water – that great River of God – and hewn for themselves broken cisterns incapable of holding water. The danger that we should do the same is very real.

The River of Grace runs powerfully through Scripture, but needs our permission to run into and through our lives.

[1] Isaiah 12:3; 44:3; Psalm 42:1; Zechariah 13:1; 14:8.
[2] Jeremiah 2:13.

16

Time to break cover

The name Nicodemus crops up repeatedly in Jewish history. It was a given name passed down the generations of one of the most aristocratic of Jewish families. The Nicodemus who came to Jesus by night was almost certainly a member of that family.[1]

Hence, perhaps, the surprising thing is not that Nicodemus came to Jesus by night, but that he came at all.

Not only was Nicodemus an aristocrat, but an influential one. When Jesus died, Nicodemus accompanied Joseph of Arimathea to the office of Pontius Pilate to ask permission to bury the body. To negotiate with Pilate was no big deal; members of the family of Nicodemus had negotiated on behalf of the whole nation and would do so again.[1] What *was* a big deal was that Joseph and Nicodemus, both members of the Jewish ruling council, the Sanhedrin, were accepting – for all to see and hear – the reproach of being disciples of Jesus.[2]

Much earlier, Nicodemus had used his considerable standing on the seventy-member Sanhedrin to plead for the just treatment of Jesus. He did so immediately after a fellow Pharisee had said that no one of his party (or any other) had any time for Jesus, and that his support was exclusively from 'the mob'. When Nicodemus had made his plea, he was asked, sarcastically, 'Are you from Galilee too?'[3]

But, as the months went by, that situation changed. It was not that many prominent persons came out openly in favour of Jesus. They were too afraid of being 'put out of the synagogue', and all the odium that would be attached to that.[4] Hence they became 'undercover' disciples.

It took Golgotha to make Nicodemus break cover. Think of that. At the moment when the stigma of being a disciple had never been greater, when most of the regular disciples of Jesus were behind bolted doors 'for fear of the Jews', when John and a handful of women tearfully looked up at the corpse of Christ hanging above them – *at that precise moment*, Nicodemus and his friend Joseph broke cover and became open supporters of the cause of the Nazarene!

When other disciples were crushed, their hopes dashed, Nicodemus and Joseph walked from Skull Hill back to the city and sought an interview with the governor.

Pilate gave his permission to the two distinguished Jewish leaders. I wonder what sense he made of their support? I wonder what Caiaphas, Annas and all the rest did and with what words they consigned Nicodemus and Joseph to social, spiritual and political oblivion?

I hope Joseph, Nicodemus, John and the women had help getting the body of Jesus down from the cross. Joseph was to provide the 'new tomb, in which no one had ever been laid'.[5] What did Nicodemus do? He 'brought a mixture of myrrh and aloes, about seventy-five pounds'. And then? 'The two of them wrapped [the body], with the spices, in strips of linen', according to Jewish custom, and placed it in the new tomb nearby.[6] 'The women . . . followed Joseph and saw the tomb and how [the] body was laid in it.'[7] A 'great stone' was placed at the entrance and – at the Sanhedrin's request but Pilate's orders – the tomb was sealed and secured, and an armed guard was put in place.[8]

When we take a second look at the 'seventy-five pounds' of myrrh and aloes Nicodemus provided, we discover that he was not a man for half measures. He was giving Jesus a burial fit for a king. Literally.[9] Was Nicodemus trying to make up for the understated support he had given Jesus while he was alive?

Where was Nicodemus coming from?

Why did Nicodemus wait until Jesus had died to come out in support?

The journey of Nicodemus had begun with that night-time visit to Jesus. When Jesus was approached by Nicodemus, he was not only being approached by a man of great social and political importance, but by a leading theologian.

When Nicodemus failed to grasp the second-birth teaching of Jesus, Jesus asked him, 'Are you *the* teacher of Israel and do not understand these things?'[10]

Jesus was referring to the impressive credentials of Nicodemus. He was a top theologian: what we would call 'the leading expert on the Old Testament'. Jesus was saying, 'You're Israel's leading scholar and you haven't come across the new birth teaching in the Scriptures?'

That was where the spiritual journey of Nicodemus began. It was not that he had been ignorant of the Old Testament. It was just that he had not begun to understand key passages.

Jesus had challenged his assumption that entry to the Kingdom of God was possible because of racial inheritance, energetic law-keeping, Scripture knowledge and acts of piety. Jesus was saying, That's not it at all. And Jesus was appealing to the Scriptures as the basis for what he was teaching.

John 3:1-15 contains only an outline summary of the Jesus-Nicodemus discussion.

How would Jesus have supported his 'new birth from above' teaching?

Without question, he would have referred Nicodemus to Ezekiel 36:25-27.

In verse 25 God offers to wash us clean from the disfiguring dirt of sin. Then, in verse 26, he continues, 'I will give you a new heart and put a new spirit in you; I will remove from you your heart of stone and give you a heart of flesh. And I will put my Spirit in you. . . .' I can almost hear Jesus saying, 'New birth "of water and of the Spirit" – don't you *see*, Nicodemus?'

And I believe that, there and then, Nicodemus *began* to see.

His journey of discovery was underway. What he had thought was important was not nearly as important when he realised that required radical surgery: a heart transplant!

In the months that separated the night-time discussion from the scene at the cross, the understanding of Nicodemus would have grown.

There is a lot in Ezekiel on the second-birth theme. Ezekiel sees a huge area covered by unburied human bones picked clean by the birds of prey and bleached white by the sun. There's not a trace of the recognisable people they had been and were meant to be. Until, that is, God breathed life into them. 'Breath entered them; they came to life and stood up on their feet – a vast army.'[11]

Ezekiel had another wonderful picture of new life.[12] The prophet saw a trickle of water flowing eastward from the Jerusalem temple. Unaccountably, it grew in volume out of all proportion as it flowed like a mighty river over the lunar Lo Debar landscape of the Wilderness of Judea – until it poured like Niagara Falls down into the Dead Sea, bringing it to life. On the banks of the River of God erupted great orchards of fruit trees.

The word grace is not used in connection with either of Ezekiel's pictures. But they represent two vivid pictures of God's grace at work. New life through the unmerited initiative of God.

As the months passed, the studies of Nicodemus would have taken him to Zechariah. Zechariah saw a picture of the river's source erupting as a fountain in the Jerusalem of the future to cleanse men and women from sin and uncleanness.[13]

But only as Nicodemus stands watching Jesus die does everything fall into place. . . . *'He was pierced for our transgressions, he was crushed for our iniquities; the punishment that brought us peace was upon him, and by his wounds we are healed. . . . He was led like a lamb to the slaughter. . . .'*[14]

At Calvary Nicodemus has witnessed the eruption of the Fountain which is the Source of the River of Grace.

His hands pierced for the wrong things my hands have done. His feet spiked for the wandering ways my feet have trod. His brow thorn-crushed for the wrong thoughts my mind has harboured. His heart broken for the wrong things my heart has loved.

Nicodemus now knows new birth experientially. His dry bones live. The desert of a scholar's life burgeons with blossoming orchards.

New birth literally means 'born from above'. The initiative is God's. But we need to *respond* to his grace.

Until we grasp God's grace there is no cleansing, no new responsive heart and no indwelling Spirit to promote our growth in grace.[15]

As with Nicodemus, our new birth begins at the foot of the cross. It is what the Holy Spirit does in our lives when we grasp God's grace.

Big deal?

The biggest Deal of all!

The only Deal that can save us eternally.

It's time to break cover!

1 William Barclay, *The Gospel of John* (St Andrew Press), vol 1, page 123.

2 Colin G. Kruse, *Tyndale New Testament Commentaries: JOHN* (IVP), page 373.

3 John 7:45-52.

4 John 12:42, 43.

5 John 19:41.

6 John 19:39-41.

7 Luke 23:55.

8 Matthew 27:62-66.

9 Kruse, *op cit*, pages 373, 374; Andrew T. Lincoln, *The Gospel According to John: Black's New Testament Commentaries* (Hendrickson), pages 484-487.

10 John 3:10, NASB.

11 Ezekiel 37. See verse 10.

[12] Ezekiel 47:1-12.
[13] Zechariah 12:10; 13:1; 14:8.
[14] Isaiah 53:1-7.
[15] Ezekiel 36:25-27.

17

Being gracious is more important than being right

The world is weary of Christians who are certain they are right but in whom there is no grace. The prodigal sons and daughters will return to the Far Country rather than enter the Father's House if they meet the elder brothers and sisters before they meet the Father.

There is only one thing the Church can give to the world that the world cannot get anywhere else – and that is grace. If the Church is not a means of grace to the world, then the Church does not serve a useful purpose from the Father's standpoint.

If the elder brothers and sisters – with their rules, rituals and dress codes – encounter the returning prodigals first, the appeal of the pigpen will suddenly improve. At least they are accepted and at home there!

That breaks the heart of the Father more than even the first departure of the prodigal. It means that someone presuming to represent him has slammed the outer door of his house in the face of a returning prodigal. Few, if any, will ever knock again when they have been rebuffed. Jesus reserved his fiercest denunciations for those who shut the door of the sheepfold on the lambs seeking to enter (the young-in-faith intent on becoming part of God's family). The Good Shepherd leaves the ninety-nine who are in the fold and risks rocky-mountain hazards to reach one lost lamb. Woe betide those who turn lambs away from the sheepfold, make it hard for them to enter or to remain.[1]

God has a right to expect that Christians, because they are part of his family, will carry his likeness. They need to shine in a darkened world. 'Theological rightness should be more than correct doctrines. It should demonstrate a vibrant relationship with God, "a visibly better product", and be offered attractively and compassionately.'[2]

Being a Christian has got to make a difference. It's not enough to have the truth. The world has to be able to see that we have internalised it and that it has changed us for the better.

'God saved you by his special favour when you believed. And you can't take credit for this; it is a gift from God. Salvation is not a reward for the good things we have done, so none of us can boast about it. For we are God's masterpiece. He has created us anew in Christ Jesus, so that we can do the good things he planned for us long ago.'[3]

Do you know how you can tell who are saved?

They have received grace *and, therefore, they are gracious.*

Grace makes a difference. It *has* to!

Churches are not places that exist to keep you healthy but sinful, or to make you rich, or to provide a little demi-world where you can strut your stuff. The church is a means of grace to the world. A congregation whose members are ungracious, aggressive, fanatical or legalistic is a failing church.

People who believe they are saved by performance are cowards. They suspect that if they accept the idea of salvation by grace through faith that Jesus will want to interfere in their lives.

And they suspect rightly!

The new-birth experience comes to those who, in repentance, reach out and grasp forgiveness and grace.

Those who grasp grace get miracles.

'If anyone is in Christ, he is a new creation; the old has gone, the new has come!'[4]

Grasping grace does not mean that you will live happily ever after. Grasping grace does not inoculate you against pain and suffering. Grasping grace and forgiveness from God does, however, make you gracious.

Why did Jesus come?

'To all who received him . . . he gave the right to become children of God. . . . From the fullness of his grace we have all received one blessing after another. . . . The law was given through Moses; grace and truth came through Jesus Christ.'[5]

Some of those who return to the Father's House take up occupancy but give nothing in return. They accept the Father's grace as if it is their right, but do nothing to show their love for him. Others of those who return embrace what the Father has done and is doing, and show their gratitude by trying to be what he wants them to be.

The first child grows further and further away from the Father. Even those outside the home know he brings discredit on all family values.

The second child grows nearer and nearer to the Father. Outsiders are attracted and want to become part of the family.

Both are children of God *in a sense*, but their ideas of what it means to be children of God are very different. The second child has become a child of God in a way foreign to the first.

'From the fullness of his grace. . . .' The word used for fullness is *pleroma*: it is the sum total of all that is God. In Jesus there was the totality of God's grace. We can go to Jesus with any need and find it supplied. The grace of God in Jesus is inexhaustible. Those who draw on God's grace become gracious and find salvation.

The Bible says there is no other way to be saved than by the grace of God. It also says that once we have received God's grace we ourselves must be gracious. Why? Because we are to be God's conduits of grace to the world.

And that, I fear, is where the formula breaks down in too many cases.

Ungracious people are not winsome. The number one problem of the Church is not church growth, but church health. But church growth and church health are linked. Growth is stunted because so many of us are ungracious.

Paul speaks of 'a remnant chosen by grace'.[6] And means? A

loyal minority who, having received God's grace and been saved by grace, *behave graciously*. It's basic. It's very, *very* basic! 'The fruit of the Spirit is love, joy, peace, patience, kindness, goodness, faithfulness, gentleness and self-control.'[7] And the only word that comes within a mile of encompassing *all* those virtues is grace.

Paul gives this advice about outreach: 'Live wisely among those who are not Christians, and make the most of every opportunity. Let your conversation be gracious and effective so that you will have the right answer for everyone.'[8]

That applies to all of us. The Bible makes no exceptions. No one is exempt on account of trade, profession, income, gender, race, creed, colour or camouflage. Grace and graciousness: the irreducible, non-negotiable minimum.

It is not enough to have the truth. It is not enough to be right. The truth must manifest itself through the quality of your relationship with God. The truth about grace makes you gracious. Being gracious makes you an attractive, compassionate representative of Jesus in the world.

The world *is* tired of Christians who say that they have the right beliefs but in whom there is no grace.

Grace *is* the one commodity the Church has on offer that the world cannot get anywhere else.[9]

Grasp grace – and be gracious!

Grace is not simply leniency when we have sinned. Grace is the enabling gift of God to conquer sin. Grace is power, not just pardon.

[1] Matthew 18:1-14; 23:1-36.
[2] Cynthia Benz, unpublished PhD dissertation accepted by the University of Birmingham, 2004, page 164.
[3] Ephesians 2:8-10, NLT.
[4] 2 Corinthians 5:17.
[5] John 1:12, 16, 17.
[6] Romans 11:5, 6, KJV, NKJV, NIV, NRSV.
[7] Galatians 5:22, 23.
[8] Colossians 4:5, 6, NLT.

[9] John Ortberg makes a powerful case for this in his brilliant, insightful book *Love Beyond Reason* (Zondervan), chapter 8.

18

Grace as power

Joseph experienced grace as empowerment.

His was a rollercoaster of a life.

His father Jacob had had children by four different women and produced, unsurprisingly, a very large and dysfunctional family.

Joseph came towards the younger end of the age range. His mother, Rachel, had always been his father's favourite. Nevertheless, Jacob and Rachel had been trying for a family for years before Joseph was born. When, some time later, Rachel bore Benjamin, it proved to have been a birth-too-far. She died.

When Rachel died, all that was left of the love of Jacob's life was Joseph and his baby brother.

Joseph grew up adored, protected and pampered by his father. Jacob's unmistakeable favouritism made Joseph's status within the family a source of conflict.

Among Joseph's eleven brothers were men twenty and more years older than he. Their muscled bodies had been built on hard labour to generate a living for the family.[1] Adult males, some of them married with families, were inevitably going to take issue with favour shown to a mere adolescent.

At 17 Joseph appears as a tale-bearing father's favourite, naive, unfeeling and more than a little insufferable. Out of a gifted son, bad parenting was making a monster, and a victim of his brothers' envy. At some level Jacob seems to have been aware of this.[2]

The foolish young Joseph showed no signs of the wise, sagacious ruler who would superintend the Egyptian economy years later.

Jacob might have seen the leadership possibilities in Joseph. He presented him with the long princely robe that marked him out as a member of the leisured classes as distinct from the sons of toil who were his brothers. It is significant that the only other place in which the Scriptures mention a 'richly ornamented robe' is with regard to the garb of a royal princess.[3]

Could Jacob have been more tactless?

Joseph was seventeen, it was reasonable for his brothers to expect that he would take his share of the hard work. The encampment in which they all lived became a bitter, unhappy place. The brothers didn't have a kind word for Joseph.

But worse was to come. Joseph began to dream dreams of greatness. Worse still. He told his brothers and parents all about them.

The first dream's transparent meaning was that one day a princely Joseph would receive obeisance from his brothers.

The second dream's equally transparent meaning was that Joseph's parents, as well as his brothers, would do obeisance to him. That was too much even for Jacob![4] The second dream might have had its origins in an insolent pride on Joseph's part that needed to be humbled.

Be that as it may, Joseph's brothers resolved to take drastic action to prevent either dream from achieving reality.

With their flocks, Joseph's brothers travelled north to Shechem and, from thence, to Dothan. That was sixty-five miles from the family encampment. Foolishly, Jacob sent Joseph for news of them. When they saw in the distance the richly garbed talebearer, the ten older brothers devised a plan to murder him. That plan was abandoned when a group of camel-borne merchants en route to Egypt from Gilead came by.

The brothers stripped Joseph of his princely robe and sold him as a slave to the merchants for twenty shekels. What was the point of spilling brotherly blood when they could make some money?

chapter eighteen

Joseph was taken to Egypt as a slave.

The princely robe was dipped in an animal's blood and was presented to Jacob as evidence that Joseph had been killed by a wild beast.

Jacob went into mourning and refused to be comforted.

So where was the Hand of Grace in all this?

Not in evidence. Yet.

Joseph was learning some overdue lessons to correct the consequences of poor parenting.

We next meet him in an Egyptian slave market, in the worst of circumstances. But God uses the worst of circumstances in which to perform his greatest miracles of grace. Joseph was a broken person; and God can rebuild and empower broken people.

Joseph was being put in place to play a pivotal part in the history of nations. He needed to grow up and, by God's grace, he did. To assist the maturity process, God needed Joseph away from his doting dad and malicious brothers.

God was not responsible for either. Nor was God responsible for their foolish and evil actions. But God knows that trust develops through trials. Another word for trust is faith. And faith was the making of Joseph.

The sentence 'The Lord was with Joseph' is repeated again and again in the narrative. Of course, the Lord had been with him before he was sold as a slave in Egypt. But it was when every other support was removed that Joseph noticed his presence and established a close, bilateral relationship with him. Joseph began to experience grace as more than an abstraction. It became power: a means to maturity.

Joseph was sold to Potiphar, the captain of Pharaoh's elite guard. That guard was, among other things, Pharaoh's execution squad.

From the merest domestic, Joseph was promoted by Potiphar to be head of his household. His increased visibility brought him into contact with Potiphar's wife. The narrative continues, 'Now Joseph was well-built and handsome.' That might have been why Joseph became the subject of an indecent proposition.

God's empowering grace enabled Joseph to reply, 'My master has withheld nothing from me except you, because you are his wife. How then could I do such a wicked thing and sin against God?'[5]

Potiphar's wife kept up the pressure day after day. Joseph staunchly resisted her propositions. So staunchly, in fact, that she felt insulted. Soon she responded with a false accusation of sexual assault and attempted rape.

They weren't soft on crime in ancient Egypt. Joseph was a slave; whatever the verdict, he had to accept it. And Potiphar, who gave the verdict, was chief executioner. The fact that Potiphar permitted imprisonment in place of the death penalty owed much to the respect Joseph had won. It might also have owed a little to misgivings 'about the full accuracy of the charge'.[6] However, those misgivings did not save Joseph from the deepest, darkest dungeon and, if he suffered from moments of self-pity in his growth-in-grace process, he might have reflected that he had exchanged an instant death for a slow one.

However, 'God was with Joseph' in the dungeon, too. God's presence and his grace were not passive. God was blessing Joseph in an active way. When two senior officers from Pharaoh's household were suspected of treasonable intent, they found Joseph was the man in charge down in the dungeon. When they asked if he could help interpret their dreams, Joseph said, 'I can't; but God can.' When the case of one of the men turned out well, and he was restored to his old position at court, Joseph said, 'Remember me!'

He did. But not until two years later. It was then that Pharaoh had a momentous dream that his 'wise men' were unable to decipher.

Joseph was brought to the attention of the Pharaoh of Egypt. With God's help he interpreted the dream and, by God's grace, a day that began in a dungeon ended with Joseph's appointment as Egypt's Minister of Economic Affairs.

David left the Cave of Failure to be King.

Joseph left the Dungeon of Injustice to become Pharaoh's

Number Two.

The reason that Joseph's appointment was an outstanding success rather than an embarrassing failure was that God had used his slavery and imprisonment to make a man of him, and a great one at that. Grace is more than pardon. It is power – to grow, to mature, to realise the potential God saw at the first.

[1] Read the story in Genesis 35:16 through to the end of Genesis 37. On how Jacob and his sons made their living, see John C. L. Gibson, *GENESIS*, vol. 2 (St Andrew Press), pages 229-231.
[2] Genesis 37:9-11.
[3] Gibson, *op cit*, page 227. See also 2 Samuel 13:18.
[4] See Genesis 46:29.
[5] Genesis 39:9.
[6] Derek Kidner, *GENESIS: An Introduction and Commentary* (IVP), page 191.

19

The rainbow of grace

During his years in prison, to what extent do you think Joseph was aware of the Hand of Grace in his life?

For sure he could not have known precisely what God was seeking to accomplish.

Nevertheless, it was by means of Pharaoh's dream, and of Joseph's interpretation of it, that God was able to save Egypt from mass starvation. Foreknowledge of fourteen years of unusual climatic conditions and Pharaoh's astute appointment of Joseph as his Head of Economic Planning made possible the storage of grain in vast silos during the seven years of plenty, so that in the seven years of famine not just Egypt but the nations around could be saved. And they included Canaan, where the elderly Jacob and his eleven sons were still eking out a living.

As a slave and in prison, all that Joseph had known – and all that he had needed to know – was that 'the Lord was with him'. The same assurance is available to us during the hard times. The Lord is God of the tough times as well as the times of plenty.

For lengthy periods, life can be downright unfair. God knows that from personal experience. God in Christ shared the common ups and downs of life with us. Christ gained the victory for himself and for those who trust in him. That is why Scripture contains this uncompromising promise: 'We know that God will make everything that happens to us in this life come out to our eventual good, as long as we trust him and remain true to the purpose for which he called us.'[1]

The *garda* chopper pilot was shouting and animated when he landed. We assumed he'd sighted a suspect. In fact, when we made sense of his words through the din of the helicopter blades, we found that he was shouting, *'Rainbows are round!'* The majesty of that fact had killed his interest in the suspect. With finger pointing and arm extended he was defining a circle: *'Round! Not just an arc, but a circle!'*

Weather conditions over Dundalk had been a typically Irish mix of bright sunshine, dark cloud and rain squalls. Above Dundalk, in all of that, the police pilot had reached just the right spot in the heavenly prism and had seen the whole circle of the rainbow, not just the arc visible to the earthbound. For him it had been a once-in-a-lifetime moment!

It is not just in Ireland that rainbows are round.

In the latter part of his life, Joseph glimpsed, by God's grace, the whole picture. By then his father was dead and, with his brothers, he had been back to Canaan to bury him. On their return to Egypt Joseph's brothers were nervous. Would he act vengefully towards them? Pay them back for all the wrong they had done him in the early years?

God's grace enabled Joseph to see the whole picture. He extended that grace by sharing it with his brothers. Revealing all that had happened, he said: *'You meant evil against me; but God meant it for good. . . .'*[2]

He had glimpsed the rainbow circle.

God had taken his brothers' wrong actions and wrong motives – betrayal, slavery, jealousy – and had used the circumstances to bless Joseph and the people. By the Lord's placing Joseph in a powerful position and, through dreams, giving him shafts of insight, God had been enabled to avert mass starvation which would have destroyed Egypt and many other people groups in the Middle East, including the family of Jacob.

What a wonderful insight into the way God operates!

Again and again God takes the trains of events that men set in motion (from who knows what appalling motives) and uses them to bring about good.

During the seven years of famine, Joseph's brothers had come to him for food. So many were the years that had passed, and so astonishing was the way powerful Egyptians were dressed and made up, that they had not recognised him. To ascertain whether they, too, had matured Joseph set some elaborate tests. Then, inevitably, there came the moment when he said, 'I am your brother Joseph, the one you sold into Egypt.' Then *immediately* he had added: 'Do not be distressed and do not be angry with yourselves for selling me here, because it was to save lives that God sent me ahead of you. . . . God sent me ahead of you to preserve for you a remnant on earth and to save your lives by a great deliverance.'[3]

But that glimpse of the big picture had been too much for Joseph's brothers. Either they had not been able to take it in or it had seemed too good to be true.

That's how it is with God's great, limitless grace. Having fed his brothers and their families from the Egyptian bounty and, subsequently, given them lands and pastures in Egypt's most fertile region, Joseph had to reassure them after his father's death:

'Don't worry. The past is past. God had a purpose in it all.'

That was what they had not taken on board. The prodigal brothers had received Joseph's embrace. But, like the older brother in Christ's story, they had not yet entered the party. They were offered forgiveness, but had not accepted it. They had sidestepped the conversion experience.

There are millions of *persona non grata* (people without grace) in the Church, too. Having failed to grasp that grace is *gratis*, they look for ways to pay for it and, finding none, they never actually receive it. And not having received grace, they become legalistic and ungracious. Not only do they not have the fruit of the Spirit, but are incapable of recognising it.

'For it is by grace you have been saved, through faith, . . .' Paul insisted.[4] And faith was not home-grown, but God's gift.

In God's great scheme of things, the power, lust, ambition and caprice of man does not have the last word in shaping events. That is one of the great themes of Scripture: 'In the word of God the curtain is drawn aside, and we behold, behind, above, and through all the play and counter-play of human interests and power and passions, the agencies of the all-merciful One, silently, patiently working out the counsels of his own will.'[5]

On trial before Pontius Pilate, Jesus chose, for quite long periods, to be silent. At one stage, frustrated, the Roman barked:

'Are you not speaking to me? Do you not know that I have power to crucify you, and power to release you?'[6]

Never forget the reply of Jesus. It has a significance way beyond the immediate situation. It is true for your situation and mine:

'You would have no power over me if it were not given to you from above.'

All the troubles that happen to you must first be sieved through the great grace of our sovereign God. And, even then, Satan (the initiator of your troubles) has to contend with the fact that the all-merciful One will silently, patiently, cause them to work together for good as long as you trust him. Ever thought how galling that must be for the devil?

The devil's greatest victory was his biggest defeat.

At Calvary Satan thought he had the *dramatis personae* just where he wanted them. The Romans were being cruel, the scribes were being scornful, and the Son of God was being tortured to death.

Mel Gibson's film, *The Passion*, captures Satan's presence at – and enjoyment of – Calvary. His supreme exultance is when Christ dies in agony. Then the perspective changes – and so does the expression on Satan's face. Gibson's camera angle makes it look as if Satan is already in the bottomless pit. A way out has been made for man, and Satan knows he has fire in his future. The moment of Satan's greatest victory was, in fact, the instant of his final, irreversible defeat.

Salvation was accomplished. The veil of the temple was torn. The devil was done for.

The future and the past met in Calvary's present and God's eternal NOW.

From the foot of the Cross we can invite God to heal any brain-stored pictures of the past that damage our present. God can heal our memories, the source of more of our problems than we care to admit. From the foot of the Cross we can invite God to step into our future and we can leave it with him without worry. He can handle our tomorrows, the source of many of our anxieties.

From the foot of the Cross we can reach out from our present and receive salvation and, with it, assurance, the Peace of Jesus.

The death, resurrection and ascension of Jesus complete the rainbow circle.

Look at John's description of Heaven's throne room: 'In my vision I saw a throne had been set up in Heaven, and there was someone seated upon the throne . . . and *all around the throne* shone a halo like an emerald rainbow.'[7]

Notice: *All* around the throne.

Jesus promised: ' "What I am doing you do not understand now, but you will know after this." '[8]

What is happening to you now you may not understand. 'But,' says Jesus, 'trust me. All will be made plain one day. Before the throne the picture will be complete.'

We see only part of the rainbow now. From the Cross, by faith, we can catch glimpses of the whole. But only from eternity's perspective – before the throne of God – will the whole picture be visible.

Then the rainbow will be round. Only then will there be more answers than questions.

[1] Romans 8:28, *Clear Word*.
[2] Genesis 50:20, NKJV.
[3] Genesis 45:4-7.
[4] Ephesians 2:8.

[5] *Education*, page 173.

[6] John 19:10, NKJV.

[7] Revelation 4:2, 3, Phillips. Italics mine.

[8] John 13:7, NKJV.

20

The prodigal daughter story

Sometimes the scandal of grace becomes a literal, talk-of-the-town scandal. That's how it was with Gomer.

When the golden age of David and Solomon was a distant memory and the kingdom had broken in two, God's people lapsed into long centuries of unfaithfulness and degeneracy. The prophets were ignored, or on occasion gruesomely murdered. The kings were no better than their people. It was clear that, not far into the future, the fragments that remained of a once great kingdom would fall prey to one of the powerful but brutal empires of the East and that the people themselves would be dragged off into the huge slave gangs the Eastern despots used to build their cities.

All that could save God's unfaithful people was repentance followed by reform.

God tried one last-chance-saloon strategy to bring that about. He called a prophet who would do more than be his mouthpiece. He would see through God's eyes and feel something of what God felt.

God called a prophet who was commanded not just to speak for God but to demonstrate God's love for all to see. If the people could watch God's heartbreak and know how much he still loved them and wanted to transform them by his grace – then surely, *surely*, they would grasp his grace.

God called Hosea to marry a woman – Gomer – who would

become first a promiscuous and unfaithful wife and finally a prostitute.

When Hosea married Gomer she was an ordinary Israelite woman.[1] But she was unfaithful from the first. Three children were born; their paternity is – and probably always was – uncertain. The names chosen for them speak volumes.

Hosea lived out his heartbreak as Gomer went from lover to lover. The people were invited to see that heartbreak as a reflection of the anguish of God at the unfaithfulness of his people. The language Hosea used on behalf of God was shocking. At times we recoil in revulsion. One thing we cannot do is read it with complacency and detachment. That is just not an option.

But throughout the book of Hosea we have a picture of God deeply distraught by our sin, but even more deeply reluctant to carry out his threats. Parents will recognise that feeling. God storms, pleads, shocks, cajoles – but, astonishingly, fails to make an impact on the people of Israel!

Gomer's corrupt sexuality becomes a figure of fallenness, and a vehicle to display the sins of the whole nation. Not only the *women* of the nation. Not even *primarily* the women of the nation. *The whole nation.*

The sharpness of God's pain reflected in his complaints was directly related to the majesty of the Person who was suffering. Husbands and wives and especially fathers and mothers know acute pain. It exceeds all that a shepherd would feel for a sheep, a judge for a defendant or a king for his subjects. God feels that pain for which there is no balm or panacea. Not until Jesus weeps over Jerusalem, endures the pain of betrayal, complains from the Cross, 'My God, Why have you forsaken me?' do we have a clearer picture of wounded majesty than in Hosea.

Away from home, Gomer sank to what appeared to be the depths of degeneration; but then she fell further. She lost her freedom. Finally, she became a hardened, vicious object whom nobody wanted.

Gomer was put up for auction there in the centre of the town where everyone knew her story. Who will buy? How much is she worth? What *is* the value of a soul?

In *The Mayor of Casterbridge*, Thomas Hardy told a story based on a real-life event in which a drunken man sold his young wife to a sailor for five guineas.

When the Abolition of Slavery Act went through in 1833, it was calculated that the average market value of a slave was £37.

In Gomer's time, as in Christ's, the value of a slave was said to be thirty pieces of silver.

A dreadful auction, then, in a town's market place. Prostitutes for sale. Red-faced men, too intoxicated to stand without support; the air blue with their ribald remarks. The attractive wenches were sold first. Then those well past their sell-by dates who fetched a much lower price.

Finally, there was one haggard, worn-out woman whom nobody wanted. Years of low living had taken their toll. Once she had been in great demand, but no one wanted her now. Was Gomer too hard for tears?

She had once had a husband. A man of God. He had lived miserably because of her unfaithfulness. She had left him to be father and mother to those children.

Hosea, home alone, had a word from the Lord: 'Go; show your love to your wife again. . . . Love her as the Lord loves the Israelites. . . .'[2]

Back in the marketplace Gomer was still on the auction block. There were still no takers. Her hard gaze settled on a figure shouldering his way to the front of the crowd. Looked familiar. What was he shouting?

'I'll take her! How much?'

'She's a special! Half price!' responded the auctioneer. 'Fifteen pieces of silver and a homer and a half of barley!' The jeering stopped when everyone recognised Hosea. There was silence.

Gomer was bought back by her husband.

God hates the sin. God loves the sinner. The language of severity in Hosea gives way to the language of tenderness. The Valley of Trouble had been made into a gateway of hope.[3]

For every prodigal son and daughter there is a door of hope. It swings wide into the light and warmth of the Father's home.

The anguish that created that door of hope was not Gomer's or the prodigal's or Israel's. It was the Prodigal Father's. ' "Oh, how can I give you up, Israel? How can I let you go? . . . My heart is torn within me," '[4] God says.

Would you have done what Hosea did? Bought Gomer back?

God told Hosea: Go; do what I do.

God did it. In Jesus. Jesus is God spelling himself out in language we can all understand.

God sees possibilities in you and me that even we cannot see. He says, 'How can I give you up? . . . How can I hand you over? . . .'[5]

God gate-crashed Hosea's life with a command, 'Go! Buy her back! Restore her! Love her – just as the Lord loves!'

Could you have done it? I couldn't. The thing is a mystery. It is the wonder of grace.

What *is* the value of a soul?

One final auction. In a garden at midnight. Jesus has been betrayed for thirty pieces of silver. Betrayed by a friend. The awful burden of our sin weighed him down. *'My Father, if it is possible, may this cup be taken from me?'* Nothing was inevitable about Gethsemane. The outcome of the auction was not predetermined. He could have wiped away the blood-sweat and left us to perish in this cesspit of sin. But he concluded, *'Yet not as I will, but as you will.'*[6]

By the time the blazing torches of the arresting party entered the olive garden, the auction was over. At Calvary the following day, the price was paid.

On Calvary Jesus paid the price of a soul. Grace costs nothing to its recipients. It cost everything to the Giver. But because of Calvary every prodigal son and daughter can choose to come home.

[1] On how to interpret Hosea read David Allan Hubbard's *Tyndale Bible Commentaries: HOSEA* (IVP) and Paula Gooder's *The People's Bible*

Commentary: HOSEA TO MICAH (The Bible Reading Fellowship).

[2] Hosea 3:1.

[3] See Hosea 2:14, 15, NLT.

[4] Hosea 11:8, NLT.

[5] Hosea 11:8.

[6] Matthew 26:39.

21

Grace: The source of the miracle

When the Cold War was at its most glacial, Scottish missionary Geoffrey Bull found himself in a prison in Mao's China. The cell was incredibly tiny, and Bull was impossibly cramped. He stayed sane by counting off the days, reciting Scripture, and reflecting on biblical passages. 'I had no Bible in my hand, no watch on my wrist, no pencil or paper in my pocket,' he wrote later. 'There was no real hope of release. There was no real hope of life. There was no real possibility of reunion with those I loved. The only reality to me was my Lord and Saviour Jesus Christ.'

All life's props had been knocked away. He had nothing except imprisoning walls. Nothing, that is, except Christ. And Geoffrey Bull made the discovery of a lifetime. He found that Christ was more than enough. 'He was everything to me . . . my fullest nourishment amidst the meagre food. . . ,' he said.

After Bull had spent nearly four years in prison, the Norwegian government negotiated his release. Then he wrote a book about his experiences titled *God Holds the Key.* In it he compares his cramped conditions with those of the infinite God when imprisoned in the flesh of a tiny baby.

• 'Think of his eyes,' he wrote. Eyes accustomed to roving across galaxies were unable to focus on his mother's face.

• 'Ponder his hands,' Bull continued. The hands that created all things, that flung stars into space, could barely grasp his mother's finger.

• Then there was the voice that 'spake and it was done' – gurgling incoherently from a mouth that dribbled.

There is no better revelation or illustration of infinite love and infinite grace anywhere than in what Christians call the Incarnation: the *enfleshment* of God in Jesus Christ.

'Christ Jesus . . . though . . . in the form of God . . . *emptied himself*, taking the form of a slave, being born in human likeness. And being found in human form, he humbled himself and became obedient to the point of death – even death on a cross.'[1]

At Bethlehem the infinite God emptied himself into the tiny helpless form of a baby. *And why?* To grow and live in our neighbourhood; in a town like ours, down a street like ours. *And why?* To reveal God and to serve man. *But to what end?*

That he might die.

The Incarnation was part of God's self-revelation. An even more important part was the cross.

The one born to be King was born in order that he might die. By whose initiative? His own. *He laid down his life.*

Even if Scripture had not said that over and over, we would know it by the manner of his death. 'Then Jesus, crying with a loud voice, said, "Father, into your hands I commend my spirit." '[2]

The first-century readers of Luke's gospel would not need me to explain why Jesus 'crying with a loud voice' was remarkable. They knew about crucifixion. They knew that no crucified man in his last moments of life *ever* cried with a loud voice – except this one! He was being asphyxiated; his voice had been squeezed out of him.

Luke's first readers knew that the loud voice of our dying Saviour represented something supernatural. It told them that the death of Jesus was not the last gasp of a victim. He cried with a loud voice; once again it was the Voice that 'spake and it was done'! It was not the voice of a helpless victim, but the Voice of the King who – even then, even there – was *choosing* to lay down his life. Greater love hath no man! What grace!

'He emptied himself!'

Jesus was rich; for our sakes he became poor.[3] Jesus was 'the very form of God' – *eternal* God – but he voluntarily surrendered his life, having taken the place of sinners, so that all sinners might choose to live in Christ. *He* chose to die that *we* might choose to live. *He* emptied himself that *we* might be full.

Paul was using the most vivid word possible to make clear the sacrifice of the Incarnation. The Greek verb *kenoun* literally means *to empty*. It is used for pouring liquid out of a container until there is nothing left.

The first Christmas was an expensive time. It cost Heaven God's Son. The first Easter was an expensive time. It cost God's Son his life.

There is one thing that the Church has to offer that the world cannot get anywhere else: *grace*.

The Church is a means of grace, or it is a waste of space. And the same holds true for every person within the Church.

The world says: You gets what you pays for! There's no such thing as a free lunch! By contrast God *emptied himself* in Bethlehem and at Calvary. Through that emptying – made possible through his birth and his death – Jesus made fullness an option for the penitent sinner, eternity a prospect, and he did it for free.

Grace is not grace unless it's *gratis*.

'The Word became flesh and made his dwelling among us. We have seen his glory, the glory of the One and Only, who came from the Father, full of grace and truth. . . . From the fullness of his grace we have all received one blessing after another. For the law was given through Moses; grace and truth came through Jesus Christ.'[4]

God became flesh and blood and moved into our neighbourhood. And from his fullness we have all received grace upon grace.

[1] Philippians 2:6-8, NRSV.
[2] Luke 23:46, NRSV.
[3] 2 Corinthians 8:9.
[4] John 1:14, 16, 17.

22

When grace comes to Roaring Camp

Sal died when her baby was born – and she had been the only woman at Roaring Camp. In the days of the Gold Rush that camp had the worst reputation of them all.

But the baby belonged to the camp. There could be no doubt about that. So he was wrapped in rags and placed in a box marked 'Whisky'.

As soon as he was placed there the men of Roaring Camp felt instinctively ashamed. One of their number was dispatched on an eighty-mile mule journey to find the best rosewood cradle money could buy.

The moment he returned, the baby was accommodated in its cradle. It was then that the rags seemed so dreadfully out of place and another man was sent on another journey – and returned with fresh white baby clothes.

Was it the clothes that showed up the filth on the floor? Whatever it was, a dozen rough gold-diggers scrubbed that floor until it was the colour of fresh-hewn pine.

Then it was clear that the filthy ceiling and walls didn't go with the clean floor. So they were whitewashed.

That showed up the broken windows; so they were mended and curtains were hung.

'S-H-H-H, . . .' the men often said. *'The baby's sleeping!'* The men kept the noise down and Roaring Camp lost the characteristic that had earned it the name.

On fine days the rosewood cradle was placed near the mine entrance. Somehow it made the whole area appear so drab that, to please the baby, a garden was planted that mixed colourful flowers with gemstones found in the mines.

Tuttle, who owned the general store nearby, saw the way the wind was blowing – and ordered in soap, shaving materials, shirts and suits. In no time he found a market for them. That would have been unthinkable before the birth of the baby!

That story was first written down by Francis Brett Hart, himself a one-time gold-miner. It was published in a book titled *The Luck of Roaring Camp*. In connection with the story of the baby, Hart adds this: 'The world itself was Roaring Camp two thousand years ago. . . . A man – every man – was either a slave owner or a slave, either a pitiless tyrant or a cringing victim. Womanhood was debased and dishonoured. Childhood was destitute of sanctity. Children, unwanted, were strangled or drowned. . . . Then a little Child was born at Bethlehem. In the presence of that little Child, men saw as they had never seen before that the world needed tidying up. The cry of the slave would not harmonise with the song of the angels. So slavery had to go. The degradation of womanhood was put to shame. And, ever since the Babe was born, childhood has been treated as a sacred thing. . . .'

'If anyone is in Christ, he is a new creation. . . .' At the heart of the Christian Gospel is the miracle of new birth. Grasp grace, and be gracious; that's the deal.

Christianity has to make a difference to us. And *we* have to make a difference to our communities.

The cry of the slave was at odds with the Christian Gospel. The abolitionist cause that triumphed over dug-in vested interests in the eighteenth and nineteenth centuries was led by Granville Sharp, John Wesley, William Wilberforce, Thomas Clarkson and John Newton. All were driven by Christian convictions.

Similarly, the iniquitous prison system in the nineteenth century was reformed as a result of the efforts of driven Nonconformists like Elizabeth Fry and John Howard. The cause of exploited children and women was taken up by great Christians, most notably Anthony Ashley Cooper, better known as Lord Shaftesbury.

For centuries, hospitals and schools have been Christian foundations. The architects of the most outstanding social reforms, including the welfare state, came from well within the Christian tradition, from Florence Nightingale and W. E. Gladstone to David Lloyd George and Nye Bevan.

Long before the Toleration Act, following the 1688 Revolution, proud Quakers like William Penn had pioneered freedom of religion and freedom of thought in the face of establishment bigotry in England.

The truism of English history is that the British reform movement owed more to Methodism than to Marx.

Jesus used the metaphors of yeast (or leaven), light and salt to illustrate the nature of the social impact he expected of the movement to which he gave rise.

'The kingdom of heaven is like yeast that a woman took and mixed into a large amount of flour until it worked all through the dough,' said Jesus.[1] Yeast, or leaven, was often linked by the Jews with an 'evil influence' such as that connected with fermentation. Before the Passover, every scrap of leaven had to be sought out from the house and burned. Jesus chose yeast or leaven as a metaphor for the Kingdom of God in order to shock and rivet attention. Yeast or leaven, Jesus knew, changed the character of the whole baking. We must never forget the power of Christ to make bad people good and good folk better. But the transformation brought about by Christianity begins only in the individual life. The transforming power of Christ and his Kingdom should be seen not just in the life of one person but in the lives of all. Christianity could and did impact the lives of women, of the vulnerable, of the weak, the sick, the aged, and the children. Jesus Christ and his Gospel represented a new force let loose upon the world.

'You are the salt of the earth. But if the salt loses its saltiness, how can it be made salty again?' asked Jesus.[2] Salt preserves and adds flavour. There should be a flavour of grace, a sparkle of joy and unselfishness about Christians that is immensely attractive. Where they are insipid, they are useless to their Lord. And, yes, salt is also connected with *purity*. The Romans said that salt was the purest of all things. Of Christians, the Lord expects standards of honesty, standards of diligence in work, conscientiousness, moral uprightness. He expects purity of speech and conduct to characterise the lives of his followers.

'You are the light of the world,' continued Jesus. 'A city on a hill cannot be hidden. . . .'[3] A light can be a warning, as with a lighthouse. Light can be warm and welcoming; as to a traveller appearing through fog or darkness. Light can guide, illuminating the road ahead. Above all, light is *visible*. It's put on a stand, not under an upturned bowl. Jesus prefers not to have undercover disciples; he is the Light of the world and, like a city on a hill, should not be hidden but reflected.

Jesus 'emptied himself, taking the form of a slave, being born in human likeness. . . . He humbled himself and became obedient to the point of death – even death on a cross.'[4]

Jesus emptied himself that we might be full *of grace*. Having grace within must make us gracious. It has to make a difference; and so have we.

John Ortberg writes, 'It was grace that was wrapped in swaddling clothes and laid in a manger. It was grace that dwelt among us, grace that healed the sick, cured the blind, and raised the dead. It was grace that partied with ragged tax collectors, grace that was called friend of sinners, grace that would not cast the first stone. It was grace that was nailed to the cross along with our sin and guilt, grace the tomb could not hold, grace that now sits on the right hand of the Father. . . .'[5]

And it is grace that calls the prodigals home, grace that shines through the Father's welcome, and grace that transforms the elder brothers and sisters so that more and more and more prodigals will want to return.

At the end of all things, it is grace that will ultimately triumph when the earth will be filled with the glory of God as the waters cover the sea.

The greatest power of all is in grace.

In the last few chapters of *What's So Amazing About Grace?*[6] Philip Yancey advances the argument that the power of grace was responsible for the massive changes that took place in the world between 1989 and 1994.

No one, says Yancey, identified the Soviet Union as the twentieth century's 'Sick Man of Europe'. Yet *rigor mortis* stiffened the muscles of the Communist Empire when no one was looking.

Then came the *annus mirabilis.*

To everyone's surprise, Poland's General Jaruzelski accepted Solidarity's victory in his country's free election.

Three months later – October 1989 – Erich Honecker was deposed in East Germany.

On 10 November demonstrators began to dismantle the Berlin Wall.

In December

– in Czechoslovakia, Vaclav Havel was elected president

– in Romania, Nicolae Ceausescu was first deposed, then shot.

The series of things that couldn't happen continued to happen for the next two years.

An attempt to topple Gorbachev in mid-1991 did not, at first, succeed. But it did precipitate the independence of the Baltic republics and the rush towards a market economy of the remainder of what had once been the USSR.

The *annus mirabilis* picked up pace in South Africa.

Nelson Mandela was released from his twenty-seven-year imprisonment on Robben Island in February 1990.

A partnership between the black majority and their historic oppressors emerged and a new democracy was created. The African National Congress won the first non-racial election in April 1994. President Mandela came to Britain to address the two Houses of Parliament. Roy Hattersley wrote:

'The mystery of why the National Party – so long in oppressive control – agreed to hand over power to the black majority may never be solved.'

At the heart of that mystery is the explanation of why the South African revolution was accomplished largely without bloodshed.

At least in part, the rapid-fire movement of the 1989-94 period had to do with the triumph of grace.

'Grace is Christianity's best gift to the world,' wrote Philip Yancey, 'a spiritual nova in our midst exerting a force that is stronger than vengeance, stronger than racism, stronger than hate.'

To Karl Barth, Jesus' gift of forgiveness – of grace – was more astonishing than Jesus' miracles. Miracles broke only the physical laws of the universe. Grace did something altogether more radical.

Grace defied the gravitational pull of self-love. Two forces are evident in the universe: gravity and grace. 'Emotionally, humans operate by laws as fixed as Newton's law of gravity. . . . All the *natural* movements of the soul are controlled by laws analogous to those of physical gravity. Grace is the only exception.'

And grace is indestructible.

Communists did their best to destroy Christianity in the many lands of the former USSR and of China. But grace is indestructible and currently those same lands represent the regions of Christianity's more rapid growth.

The destruction of the apartheid system which led to the triumph of democracy in South Africa was largely a triumph of grace over gravity.

Even if, as is claimed, Islam is 'a religion of *peace*', it is not a religion of *grace*. Nor is Buddhism, nor is Hinduism, nor is Shintoism, nor is Confucianism.

Grace is to be found only in Christianity. *And it can be had only from Christianity's Founder.*

Never has our society needed that grace more than now.

'Whatever makes us feel superior to other people . . . is gravity, not grace.'

Grace is not just the catalytic converter that brings about the transformation that is at the heart of the Gospel. Grace is also the means by which Christianity fulfils its mission of being 'the salt of the earth': the preservative agent in our country and in our world.

Never have grace-full Christians had a more important role to play.

'From the fullness of his grace we have all received one blessing after another. For the law was given through Moses; grace and truth came through Jesus Christ.'[7]

And it is the truth about grace that transforms our lives, sets us free and drives us to impact society and the world around us.

Grace transformed Roaring Camp.

[1] Matthew 13:33.
[2] Matthew 5:13.
[3] Matthew 5:14.
[4] Philippians 2:5-8, NRSV.
[5] John Ortberg, *Love Beyond Reason* (Zondervan), pages 146, 147.
[6] Millions have read Philip Yancey's *What's So Amazing About Grace?* (Zondervan) and been blessed by it. If you have time to read only one chapter, make it the last one. A number of the quotes in this chapter are taken from it.
[7] John 1:16, 17.

23

God coming through

In the ancient world, the religion of the pagan followed a set pattern. Throughout his earthly journey, he strove to earn, win or deserve a place in the afterlife. His future would be determined by the gods in their judgement after his death.

As a consequence, the world into which Jesus was born was 'dark through misapprehension of God'.[1]

But in the dark, pagan centuries, God had not been inactive. Far, far from it. The God who spoke through his Son had 'at many [former] times and in various ways' spoken through 'the prophets'.[2] 'The greatest single fact of the Christian revelation': God spoke to man, first, through the Old Testament Scriptures and, finally, 'through his Son'.[3]

The revelation of God in the Old Testament was revolutionary. Stephen Farris writes: 'Grace arches over the older testament like a rainbow.'[4] Jon Dybdahl says that 'the evidence [for that] is found, not in a few isolated proof texts, but in the very structure of the Old Testament itself. Grace is heralded in story, ritual, song and descriptions of God. It is not a minor, secondary theme, but an all-pervasive, dominant melody ringing loudly through the pages of the Old Testament.'[5] Alister McGrath argues that the basic concepts of the New Testament doctrine of salvation by grace, collectively, represent the matrix of the Old Testament.[6]

According to Stuart Tyner, in the dark, pagan world of the Old

Testament God was 'drawing his eager follower out of the quagmire of the contemporary religious scene'.[7]

At times, God did that by confronting the scene. The arguments put forward by the pseudo-friends of the suffering Job 'reek of the pagan retribution principle embedded in the . . . works-orientated religious systems' of the ancient world.[8] Through the ingenious literary structure of the book, God confounded Job's detractors who had 'obscure[d] my counsel without knowledge', expressed his anger that they had done so and pronounced Job to be right. (Job 42:3, 7.)

Pagan gods such as Molech and Chemosh demanded the sacrifice of children. On one memorable occasion God did that and, at the same time, made the strongest possible statement about the means of mankind's salvation. In doing so, he provided the most scary and dramatic narrative in the Old Testament.[9]

Sarah and Abraham, having tried for children for years, had a son – Isaac – in their old age and under miraculous circumstances. The 'son of the promise' grew to young manhood. The aged Abraham received the alarming command, clean contrary to both reason and divine promise, to sacrifice the fit, virile Isaac. The elderly man and his son made their solitary ascent of the mountain. There was the painful process in which a compliant Isaac was bound by the heartbroken Abraham on the altar. Then Heaven's last-minute intervention. And, finally, God himself provided the lamb for the burnt offering as Abraham had promised Isaac that he would.[10]

At one level this is a story of an old man being asked if he will forget self completely, to surrender everything to God, to stand before God naked and helpless, dependent solely on his grace – and not even daring to take that for granted.

At another level, countless centuries before the event, it was about the Cross. Abraham, so strong was his faith, was prepared to sacrifice his only son but was not required to. God was both willing and required to make the sacrifice of his Son when the time came. Jesus was willing to make the supreme sacrifice of himself.

With Isaac, there was the last-minute substitution of the ram.

There was no last-minute substitute for Jesus. *He* was the Substitute. When, at the foot of the mountain, Abraham and Isaac had left the servants behind, Abraham had told them, 'I and the boy will go. . . . We will worship . . . and then *we* will come back to you.'[11] Young Isaac had shared his father's faith to the extent of co-operating with him. But, at the last moment, he was released from the altar and experienced the wonder of substitutionary salvation. God himself had provided a lamb, as Abraham's faith had told him he would. Centuries later, remembering that, John the Baptist introduced Jesus with the words, ' "Look, the Lamb of God, who takes away the sin of the world." '[12]

Repeatedly in this gripping story, Isaac was referred to as Abraham's '*only* son'. In the Greek Old Testament the word *only* is translated 'beloved'. In the New Testament, at Christ's baptism and at the transfiguration, God called Jesus 'My beloved Son'.[13] 'The beloved Son was also the "only" or unique Son, for whom there could never be a substitute.'[14]

Abraham called the place of the sacrifice *Jehovah-jireh*, 'the Lord will provide'. Explaining the Cross, Christ's great champion Paul would write, 'He who did not spare his own Son, but gave him up for us all – how will he not also, along with him, graciously give us all things?'[15]

At the Cross, Jesus, God's Son, died as man's Substitute, bearing the sins of mankind, and proving once and for all that the love and grace of God are without limit. Christ suffered the death we deserve that we might enjoy the life he deserved.

The truth of God's glorious grace – and the substitutionary death enshrined in the sanctuary service – gave psalmists something to sing about and prophets something to herald and proclaim.

Isaiah was especially creative in his use of pictures of God's grace: 'You have put all my sins behind your back' (38:17). God says, ' "See, I have engraved you on the palms of my hands." ' (49:16.) 'He has clothed me with garments of salvation.' (61:10.) The Lord redeems us (63:9). Our sins are atoned for (6:7).

The greatest eloquence of Isaiah was spent on a picture of the

coming Messiah that drew on the theme of substitutionary death:
'He was despised and rejected by men,
a man of sorrows, and familiar with suffering. . . .
Surely he took up our infirmities
and carried our sorrows. . . .
But he was pierced for our transgressions,
he was crushed for our iniquities;
the punishment that brought us peace was upon him,
and by his wounds we are healed.' (53:3-5.)

God saves us as he created us – without our help.

The Christianity that is rooted in the Old Testament and blossoms fully in the New is far more about what God has done than about what we must do.

[1] *The Desire of Ages*, page 22.
[2] Hebrews 1:1, 2.
[3] Raymond Brown, *The Message of Hebrews* (IVP), page 27.
[4] Stephen Farris, *Grace, A Preaching Commentary* (Abingdon Press), page 16.
[5] Jon Dybdahl, *Old Testament Grace* (Pacific), page 16.
[6] Alister McGrath, *A History of the Christian Doctrine of Justification* (Cambridge University Press), page 5.
[7] Stuart Tyner, *Searching for the God of Grace* (Pacific), page 57.
[8] *Ibid*, page 56.
[9] John C. L. Gibson, *The Daily Study Bible: Genesis,* volume 2 (St Andrew Press), page 111.
[10] Genesis chapter 22 has been described as a 'magnificent piece of literature'. Gibson, *op cit*, page 111; D. A. Carson, R. T. France, J. A. Motyer and G. J. Wenham, *The New Bible Commentary* (IVP), page 76.
[11] Genesis 22:5. Italics mine.
[12] John 1:29.
[13] Matthew 3:17; 17:5, NKJV.
[14] J. G. Baldwin, *The Message of Genesis 12-50* (IVP), page 92.
[15] Romans 8:32.

Conclusion

The invitation of grace

Our gut instinct tells us that we must *do* something to be accepted by God. Grace responds with an emphatic 'No!' Every day we must pray afresh for the ability to hear the liberating invitation of grace.

Other gut instincts might make us behave as in a survival-of-the-fittest setting. Grace is the radical, revolutionary force that enables us to defy the gravitational pull of self-love.

God's gospel of grace is like a treasure that, in the life of an individual Christian or a community of Christians, can become buried. Those who teach Christian principles to our children often teach *un*grace: 'Heaven's gates will open wide to let good boys and girls inside.' Young people, as a consequence, give up on prayer and on God because of a mistaken belief that they have offended him by their 'disobedience, bad language or even . . . unconverted thoughts'.[1]

The 'incomparable riches' of God's grace is a treasure that needs to be taken out and examined every day.

God's grace 'expressed in his kindness to us in Christ Jesus'[2] is not just for the beginning of the Christian journey, a sort of new coat to be worn then discarded. Grace is 'the air Christians breathe in order to live'.[3]

Jon Dybdahl says, 'Grace is a free act of God to save and bless. God treats people much better than they deserve, saving them when they have done nothing to merit it. He loves and cares even when they don't.' This concept is fundamental to both testaments. Paul roots his crescendo of grace – his letter to the Romans – firmly in the Old Testament, the first four chapters containing no fewer than eleven Old Testament proof texts.[4]

At various times, the Bible either uses or is suggestive of a number of different terms – 'righteousness by faith', 'new birth', 'redemption', 'deliverance' and 'salvation' – and several different metaphors for what God does for sinners through Christ. Fundamental to all is this truth: 'God saved, saves, and always will save sinners graciously – based on his love, not on the sinner's actions.'[5]

Some Christians have been frightened of the gospel of God's grace because they have believed that it weakens commitment and compromises obedience. In fact, the opposite is the truth. When we embrace God's grace, it strengthens commitment, causes forgiveness to flourish and fuels obedience. The more we immerse ourselves in grace, the more likely we are to give grace and be gracious.

The bottom line of salvation theology: 'All have sinned, all fall short of the glory of God, and are justified freely by his grace through the redemption that came by Christ Jesus.' (Romans 3:23, 24.)

God's grace is not God's response to merit he sees in us or any actions of ours. It is original, self-initiated and unforced. God's grace is the overflow of God's love.

The invitation of grace received by M (chapter 7) was, in effect, 'Is there anybody out there? If there is, let him come to the King's table.'[6]

The invitation of grace through Isaiah is, 'Hey there! All who are thirsty, come to the water! Are you penniless? Come anyway – buy and eat!'[7]

One invitation of grace from Jesus was, 'Are you tired? Worn out? Burned out on religion? Come to me. Get away with me and you'll recover your life. . . . Walk with me and work with me – watch how I do it. Learn the unforced rhythms of grace.'[8]

The invitation of grace with which the canon of Scripture concludes is, 'Come! Whoever is thirsty, let him come; and whoever wishes, let him take the free gift of the water of life.'[9]

God is gracious. He extends the invitation of grace to all. Know that, and it will change you. Listen to the symphony of grace which plays throughout Scripture. Keep playing it over and over.

The Father issues the Invitation of Grace to prodigal sons and daughters at various stages of their experience.

Before they leave the Father's Home they may hear it. En route to the Far Country prodigals may hear the Father's voice calling after them. The true Elder Brother repeats the invitation as they squander their fortune with the fast set, though they may ignore it.

Human nature being what it is, we are most likely to hear and heed the invitation in down and broken times.

The younger son in the Jesus story heard it during his pigpen experience: no friends, no food, no self-respect, no future.

Gomer, the prodigal daughter, heard it on the auction block when she was no longer wanted by – or of value to – anyone but God.

M heard the invitation in Lo Debar, the Place of Brokenness, where he thought of himself as a no-good no-hoper. Summoned to court, he discovered that his value to the King was such that he was permanently welcome at his table.

Others needed times in dungeons of despair and caves of failure. Others had to live through long and seemingly meaningless periods during which one year was pretty much the same as the one before it. For God's grace does not just call and cleanse. It regenerates and renews, and that always takes time. Respondents to the Invitation of Grace will, having reached out and accepted it, begin an experience in which they grow in grace.

Grace is, above all things, something to be *experienced*, not just defined in the esoteric language of theology.

In the way that leads to Heaven from your house, there are two points of spiritual geography that are non-negotiable.

The first is the place where we first feel a sense of our need of the Saviour. It may be Lo Debar, M's Place of Brokenness. Or it may be more like Nicodemus's open-minded, open-hearted search that prompted him to make his initial night-time appointment with Jesus.

The second place is Calvary, the source of cleansing, regenerating and sustaining grace. There, as we 'survey the wondrous cross on which the Prince of Glory died', we acknowledge that we owe to him all that we are, do and can ever hope to be.

The focal picture in all of God's revelation of himself through Scripture is the Father in Jesus' story of the Lost Son.

The Father is not merely standing and staring down the road that comes from the Far Country, hoping to recognise the shape of the returning wastrel.

The Father, with outspread arms, is not just calling his Invitation of Grace so that whoever hears will return to the welcoming warmth of Home.

The Father through the person of the true Elder Brother has set out for the Far Country in search of sinners who are still there. And he is running.

[1] Stuart Tyner, *Searching for the God of Grace* (Pacific), page 17.

[2] Ephesians 2:7.

[3] Tyner, *op cit*, page 45.

[4] Jon Dybdahl, *Old Testament Grace* (Pacific), page 15.

[5] *Ibid*.

[6] 2 Samuel 9.

[7] Isaiah 55:1, MGE.

[8] Matthew 11:28, MGE.

[9] Revelation 22:17.